THE INVENTOR'S TIMES

REAL-LIFE STORIES OF 30 AMAZING CREATIONS

By Dan Driscoll, James Zigarelli, and the Staff of *The Inventor's Times*

THE INVENTOR'S TIMES

THE WEEKLY NEWSPAPER INVENTORS TRUST MOST

ESTABLISHED 1876

EDITORS-IN-CHIEF
Dan Driscoll
James Zigarelli

STAFF SCIENTISTS
Dr. Jiminy G. Snoof
Dr. Jiminy Snoof, Jr.
Dr. Jiminy Snoof III

STAFF LINGUISTS
Verbal T. Taylor
Lynn G. Wyst

STAFF LEGAL ADVISOR
Madge Istrate, Esq.

STAFF CONSUMER ADVOCATE
Penny Pleebo

STAFF PSYCHIC GYPSY
Magda Pantazopoulos

MANAGING EDITORS
Jason Rekulak & Paige Araujo

ART DIRECTOR
Bryn Ashburn

PHOTO EDITOR
Susan Oyama

ILLUSTRATORS
Bryn Ashburn and Christine Sheller

COPY EDITOR
Melissa Wagner

TRANSLATOR
Danielle Eduardo

MODELS
Carl Barratta, Bryn Ashburn, and Jorge Vega

QUIRK

A Quirk Book
www.quirkproductions.com

Scholastic and Tangerine Press and associated logos are trademarks of Scholastic Inc.

Published by Tangerine Press, an imprint of Scholastic Inc.; 557 Broadway; New York, NY 10012

10 9 8 7 6 5 4 3 2 1

ISBN 0-439-38474-5

Printed and bound in Singapore

THE INVENTOR'S TIMES

INTRODUCTION

WHERE WOULD WE BE WITHOUT INVENTORS?

Imagine that you lived thousands of years ago, when prehistoric men and women huddled together in damp, wet caves. Now imagine that you need to contact your friend about a hunting expedition. You leave your cave and walk all the way across the forest to your friend's cave. By the time you get there, your friend has left to gather nuts and berries. So you spend three hours carving a note on the wall. In the process, you accidentally cut your hand, and you have to wrap the wound in some muddy leaves. On your way home, you kill a rabbit for dinner, but you can't cook it because you haven't discovered fire yet. All in all, it's a pretty lousy afternoon.

Today, you would just call your friend on the telephone. You'd leave a note with a ballpoint pen. If you cut your hand, you'd put a Band-Aid on it. And you'd just throw your rabbit dinner in the microwave.

But who thought of the ballpoint pen? Whose idea was the microwave, anyway? And how exactly does a telephone work? For more than 100 years, the staff of *The Inventor's Times* has been working to answer these questions for curious readers like you.

Whenever a new invention is introduced, our writers and photographers rush to the scene to capture the whole story. Our on-staff scientists dissect each invention to learn exactly how it works. We perform "person-on-the-street" interviews to see exactly how these products will affect people's lives. And we provide advice and inspiration to anyone who wants to invent something.

If you're reading these articles, there's a chance that you could be the next Richard James (he invented Slinky), Mary Anderson (she invented windshield wipers), or Ed Lowe (he discovered kitty litter). We hope these articles give you all the information and inspiration that you need to start building your own inventions. And one day, maybe the staff of *The Inventor's Times* will be writing about you!

PHOTO CREDITS

THE INVENTOR'S TIMES

JUNE 26, 1876   VOLUME XXVI NO. 27   PRICE: ONE CENT

BELL UNVEILS NEW SPEAKING TELEPHONE

Mr. Bell addresses a spellbound audience in Philadelphia.

INVENTOR'S QUIZ

Here in Philadelphia, people are saying "hello" when they answer the phone. What will people say in other places?

1. England
2. France
3. Wild West
4. Spain
5. Italy

A. "Bonjour"
B. "Hola"
C. "Buon giorno"
D. "Cheerio"
E. "YeeeeeeeeeeeeHawwwwwww!"

Answers: 1D, 2A, 3E, 4B, 5C

IN THIS WEEK'S NEWS

"Bottled Ketchup" Is a Big Hit for Heinz

New "Bananas" Arrive in United States

Librarian Unveils "Dewey Decimal" System

VERBAL T. TAYLOR TELLS YOU

WHAT'S IN A NAME

TELE + PHONE = TELEPHONE

TELE is a Greek word meaning "distant" or "from afar"

PHONE is from the Greek word *phono*, which means "sound" or "voice"

Spectators at Centennial Exhibition Are Astonished

The inventor

PHILADELPHIA, PENNSYLVANIA– Earlier this morning, Alexander Graham Bell demonstrated an amazing new device called the "Speaking Telephone" to a crowd of dazzled on-lookers. This futuristic machine consists of two parts—a mouthpiece and a receiver—which are separated by a long electric wire. When a person speaks into the mouthpiece, his voice can be heard in the receiver!

"The day is coming when wires will be laid onto houses just like water or gas lines—and friends will converse with each other without leaving home," Mr. Bell said.

Some scientists were doubtful that Bell's contraption really worked. Franklin Parrish, who described himself as being knowledgeable in the sciences and mechanics, accused Bell of fraud. "I hear the voice with my ears," Parrish stated, "but I see that the owner of the voice is not in the room. These two facts make no sense together."

Other scientists believe that the telephone is the creation of a genius.

Alexander Bell took his first steps toward inventing his telephone as a teenager, when he discovered that a note played on a piano would be echoed by a piano in another room. Mr. Bell realized that the piano note was transmitted through the air by sound waves—and this led him to discover that sound waves, or vibrations, could be reproduced in an electrical current.

The first words spoken over the telephone occurred on March 12, after Mr. Bell spilled some battery acid in his workshop. He had raised his voice to call for his

(continued on page 2)

HOW IT WORKS

WITH PROFESSOR
JIMINY G. SNOOF

① Mouthpiece~

THIS IS THE TELEPHONE'S "EAR."

② Diaphragm~

YOUR VOICE MAKES THIS THIN DISC
OF METAL VIBRATE.

③ Metal shavings~

A LOW ELECTRICAL CURRENT RUNS
THROUGH THESE METAL SHAVINGS.
AS THE VIBRATING DIAPHRAGM
COMES INTO CONTACT WITH THE
METAL SHAVINGS, THE CURRENT
CHANGES. THE ELECTRICITY TRAVELS
OVER THE WIRE TO ANOTHER PHONE.

④ Electromagnet~

AS THE ELECTRICAL CURRENT TRAV-
ELS THROUGH THIS MAGNET, IT
MAKES THE DIAPHRAGM VIBRATE.

⑤ Diaphragm~

THE VIBRATIONS OF THE DIAPHRAGM
MOVE THE AIR AND CREATE SOUND
WAVES.

⑥ Receiver~

THIS EMITS SOUND WAVES THAT YOU
CAN HEAR.

MAKE YOUR OWN TELEPHONE!

MATERIALS:
Friend
Two plastic cups
10-foot piece of string
Pen

With two plastic cups and some string, you can create a simplified version of the telephone that doesn't require electricity. The plastic cup can capture the vibrations of your voice and send

them along the string. At the other end, the second plastic cup will act as a speaker and amplify these vibrations.

1. Using the end of your pen, carefully poke a hole in the bottom of each cup.
2. Pass the string through the hole so that the end of the string is in the cup. Tie a knot in the end of the string so it will not slide through the hole.

3. Repeat step 2 with the other end of the string, and you have a simple version of a telephone.
4. Take one cup and go to another room, so that the string is taut (but don't pull too hard). Have a friend talk into the other cup while you hold your cup to your ear. Can you hear what your friend says?

(continued from page 1)

assistant: "Mr. Watson, come here, I want you." Mr. Watson was in another room of the house, trying to repair a telephone receiver—and he was amazed when Mr. Bell's voice came out of the machine!

Many predict that the telephone will allow us to communicate with people in other houses, other cities, other states, maybe even other countries!

DID YOU KNOW?

**with Guest Expert
Ring Mybel**

In the world of inventors, a "caveat" is an announcement. Inventors will sometimes file a caveat with the United States Patent Office to announce their plans to apply for a patent. Once you file a caveat, the U.S. Patent Office will not let anyone else apply for a patent on a similar invention until you have a chance to file for your own patent.

An inventor named Elisha Gray filed a caveat just two hours after Alexander Graham Bell filed his patent for the telephone. Gray had invented a telephone, too. If he had filed two hours earlier, we would be calling Gray the "Inventor of the Telephone."

THE INVENTOR'S TIMES

DECEMBER 4, 1878   VOLUME XXVIII NO. 48   PRICE: ONE CENT

NEW TYPEWRITER IS CURE FOR MESSY HANDWRITING

Amazing "Shift" Key Allows for Capital and Lowercase Letters

ILION, NEW YORK – Four years ago, when the Remington & Sons Company unveiled a new machine called a "typewriter," the staff of *The Inventor's Times* was very skeptical. You may recall that this first typewriter was painted with flowers and looked like a sewing machine. The user had to press a foot petal to "return" the carriage to the beginning of a line. And the worst part was that it only typed in capital letters. We predicted the invention was destined for failure.

Many readers typed complaints to our criticisms. "I LIKE MY NEW TYPEWRITER," wrote Roger Perry of Pittsburgh, Pennsylvania. "I KNOW IT LOOKS LIKE I'M SHOUTING, BUT YOU GET USED TO THIS AFTER A WHILE. GIVE IT A CHANCE!"

Fortunately, Remington & Sons has just unveiled a new version of the typewriter called the "Remington 2," and it comes with a dazzling new feature called the "shift" key. The typist can use the shift key to switch between capital letters and lowercase letters. This new model isn't painted

Remington Typewriter No. 2

with flowers, either—it comes packaged in a sophisticated all-black casing.

Also new to this version is the addition of the 1 key. The original typewriter didn't have a 1 key, since Remington figured that most people could simply type the letter I and get a similar result. This decision hurt early sales, however, because many people would

(continued on page 2)

THE MAN BEHIND THE MACHINE: CHRISTOPHER LATHEM SHOLES

People have been trying to invent a typewriter since the early 1700s, but it was Christopher Lathem Sholes who made the machine a reality. Sholes worked in a Milwaukee machine shop and based his design on telegraph keys. His idea was fairly simple: when the user pressed a key, a bar would tap against a sheet of paper. Sholes put a piece of type – a raised letter – on the bar. Then he placed an inked ribbon between the bar and the paper. As a result, the bar strikes the ribbon and imprints the letter on paper. With just 26 bars, he could type every word in the English language.

Christopher Lathem Sholes

IN THIS WEEK'S NEWS

First Telephone Is Installed on the Floor of the New York Stock Exchange

John Muir Discovers the Biggest Glacier in Alaska!

Thomas Edison Creates Phonograph— What's Next?

(continued from page 1)

look at the keyboard and think that the 1 key was accidentally left off.

Alexander Swanspond, a lawyer, says that he cannot imagine using a typewriter. "In my profession, I deal with people," Swanspond says. "If I were to send out typed letters, many people would be insulted." Swanspond explained that many clients believe that typewritten mail seems impersonal. "Sometimes they won't even read it," he adds. "They assume it's garbage or junk, and throw it away."

Others claim that typewriters are boosting business. While the average person can only write 20 words every minute, experienced typists have reached speeds of more than 70 words a minute.

DID YOU KNOW?

**With Guest Expert
I. M. Ryting**
Ever wonder why typewriter keys are all over the place, instead of in alphabetical order? One rumor explains that the QWERTY layout allows new Remington salesman to type the word "typewriter" using only keys in the top row. Try it yourself!

 # LEARNING TO USE A TYPEWRITER

With practice, you can teach your fingers to "remember" the location of all the letters on a typewriter. Eventually, you'll be able to type without looking at your fingers!

To begin, put your fingers on the middle row of letters.
Left hand, from pinky to pointer finger: A, S, D, F
Right hand, from pointer finger to pinky: J, K, L, ;
Your thumbs will only press the space bar.

Practice typing sample sentences. As you touch each key, say the letter on the key out loud. Eventually you will teach your fingers to remember the correct keys.

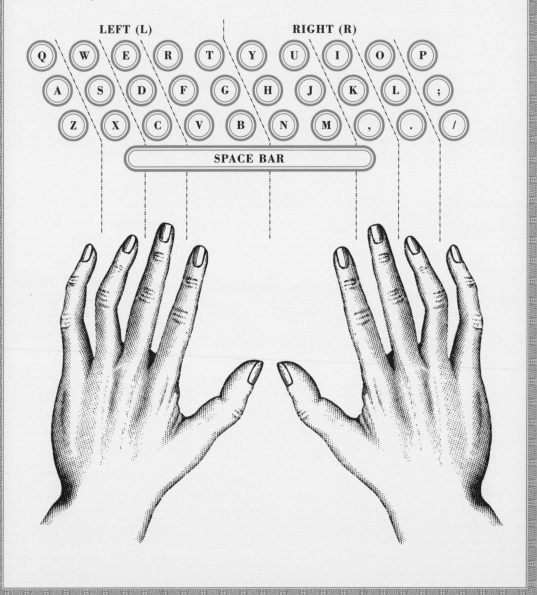

THE INVENTOR'S TIMES

OCTOBER 21, 1879   VOLUME XXIX No. 43   PRICE: ONE CENT

EDISON SEES THE LIGHT!

Electric Bulb Glows 40 Hours Straight at the Flip of a Switch

MENLO PARK, NEW JERSEY – Earlier this morning, local inventor Thomas Alva Edison announced that he has created an electric lamp that will change the way we live.

"All the problems which have been puzzling me for the last 18 months have been solved," Edison told reporters earlier today. "I expect to have every house here in Menlo Park lighted, and a number of street-lamps going within ten days."

Once Mr. Edison lights up Menlo Park, he plans to keep the electric lights burning for two weeks in order to test their effectiveness. Mr. Edison has already tested them in his laboratory. "But," he said, "I want the public to believe it from their own knowledge, and the only way to make the public believe it is to show it to them."

Thanks to this amazing invention, it seems like our days of relying on candles and gas lamps are over. But what will the big gas companies do? Every major U.S. city has

Thomas Alva Edison

miles of underground gas pipes that provide fuel for light and cooking.

(continued on page 2)

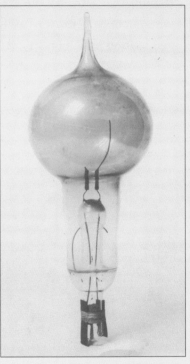

The light of Edison's life.

INVENTOR'S TIMES SURVEY

WE ASKED 3,160 INVENTORS TO PREDICT HOW MR. EDISON'S ELECTRIC LIGHT BULB WILL CHANGE PEOPLE'S LIVES.

Fear of the Boogie Man will be greatly reduced   *52%*

Other 3%

7%

Games of Hide and Seek will be much shorter

10%

Streets and public places will be safer at night

Cats' tails will no longer catch fire from candles   *28%*

IN THIS WEEK'S NEWS

Store Owners Report New "Bottled" Milk Selling Well

"Woolworth" Department Store Opens

First Steam-powered Submarine Travels 12 Miles (19 km)

(continued from page 1)

"You'll still need gas and you'll still want gas," says Hamilton G. Shlockfart, President of the New Jersey Gas Works. "This light bulb is just a fad, and when the fad goes away, we'll still be passing gas to all of our customers."

Others predict that the light bulb will replace gas altogether. Edison himself admits the future is unclear. "We are striking it big in the electric light, better than my vivid imagination first conceived," he told us. "Where this thing is going to stop, Lord only knows."

HOW DOES IT WORK?

WITH PROFESSOR JIMINY G. SNOOF

Let us now shed some light on Mr. Edison's bright idea, shall we? Here is how the light bulb works.

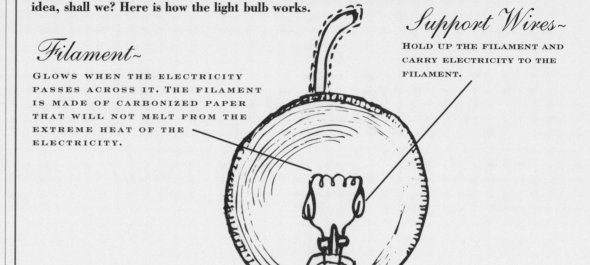

Filament~
GLOWS WHEN THE ELECTRICITY PASSES ACROSS IT. THE FILAMENT IS MADE OF CARBONIZED PAPER THAT WILL NOT MELT FROM THE EXTREME HEAT OF THE ELECTRICITY.

Support Wires~
HOLD UP THE FILAMENT AND CARRY ELECTRICITY TO THE FILAMENT.

Base~
SCREWS INTO A SOCKET WHERE ELECTRICITY FLOWS.

Glass Support~
CARRIES ELECTRICITY TO SUPPORT WIRES.

 # ON THE LIGHTER SIDE

THE PEOPLE OF MENLO PARK, NEW JERSEY, CAN'T STOP MAKING JOKES ABOUT EDISON'S NEW LIGHT BULB. HERE ARE SOME OF OUR FAVORITES:

1. How many mystery writers does it take to change a light bulb?
   Two. One to screw it almost all the way in, and another to give it a surprising twist at the end.

2. How many magicians does it take to change a light bulb?
   That depends on what you want it to change into.

3. How many fishermen does it take to change a light bulb?
   Four. One to change the light bulb, one to brag about how big the old one was, and two to brag about the one that they would have changed but "it got away."

4. How many kids does it take to change a light bulb?
   Only one. But first you have to get your parents' permission.

5. How many lawyers does it take to change a light bulb?
   How many can you afford?

The Inventor's Times

JUNE 17, 1884   VOLUME XXXIV NO. 24   PRICE: ONE CENT

NEW "ROLLER COASTER" DEBUTS AT CONEY ISLAND!

Amazing Ride Fueled by Gravity!
"Oohhhhhh Mmyyyy Gooosshhhhh!" Cries First Passenger

BROOKLYN, NEW YORK – Hundreds of kids and adults came to Coney Island yesterday to try the first "roller coaster," an amusement ride that uses gravity to race over a series of hills. Inventor LaMarcus Thompson calls his coaster the "Gravity Pleasure Switchback Railway," but most kids are referring to it as "The Coolest Thing You Will Ever Try in Your Life."

After paying five cents for

LaMarcus Thompson

admission, passengers climb the stairs of a 45-foot (14m) tower. Once at the top, they climb into a car that rests on a steel track. Attendants push the car to the edge of the first hill, and then gravity takes

Passengers on the Switchback Railway must keep all arms and legs inside the car at all times.

over. Whhhooooossshh!!! The car races up and down the track at thrilling speeds of six miles (nine km) an hour.

When the car stops, passengers exit and climb to the top of another tall tower, while ride attendants use ropes to pull the car to the top. Then everyone gets back in and rides the roller coaster back to the beginning.

Thomas Bindlebur, a ten-

year-old paperboy, waited for two hours to ride the roller

(continued on page 2)

IN THIS WEEK'S NEWS

Alaska: Now a U.S. Territory

Dr. John Harvey Kellogg Patents a "Flaked Cereal"

New Circus Calls Itself **RINGLING BROTHERS**

(continued from page 1)

coaster. "It went really fast and then my hat fell off," he said. "Have you seen my hat?"

Schoolgirl Debbie Curtis and her boyfriend, Todd Woodward, also enjoyed the ride. "You should have seen Todd's face when we came down that first hill," Curtis said. "I wish we had a photograph of our faces."

"I would pay good money for a photograph like that," she added.

DID YOU KNOW ?

with Guest Expert Moe Mentum

The Russians may have developed the earliest version of the roller coaster. In the 1600s, they used the shells of tree trunks to build long snow- and ice-covered tracks. Then they raced down these tracks on sleds made of ice. For comfort, they sat on a seat of straw.

DESIGN YOUR OWN
ROLLER COASTER

Before you can build a roller coaster, you should design a model of the track. Here's how to do it:

MATERIALS:
   A marble (the roller coaster car)
   **Heavy paper, such as oak tag or manila folders
      (the roller coaster track)**
   Tape (to connect the track)
   Cardboard tube (for a tunnel!)

1. Cut the paper into strips of track. HINT: Crease the paper lengthwise to create a "V" so the marble will not fall off the sides. Or make two lengthwise folds in the strips of paper so your track has a bottom and two "guard rails."

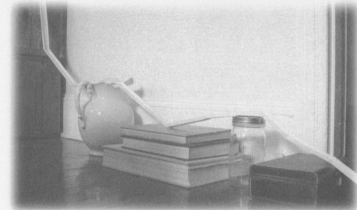

2. Tape the track together in a series of hills. The beginning of your track must be high enough for your marble to pick up a lot of speed. We recommend running the track down a flight of stairs or off the top of a couch. Then the track can race over books, boxes, pots, and pans. If you have an old garden hose in your garage, cut it into strips to add turns. (Be sure to ask a parent first.)

Here at *The Inventor's Times*, Professor Snoof has designed a coaster with jumps and loop-de-loops. Can you?

HOW IT WORKS

WITH PROFESSOR JIMINY G. SNOOF

To understand the ups and downs of roller coasters, let's consider two rules of motion that we learned from the English physicist Isaac Newton (1642–1727).

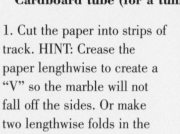

Isaac Newton

1. An object at rest will stay at rest until it is moved by an outside force.

2. Forces can change the motion of objects. An object will accelerate in the direction of a force acting upon it.

The roller coaster car is an object at rest until the attendants (*an outside force*) push it to the edge of the hill. Now it has become an *object in motion* (Rule #1).

As the car falls down the hill, the force of gravity is pulling on it, which makes the car accelerate (Rule #2). But when the car goes uphill again, it will start to slow down. This uphill section is also a force that acts against the car and slows it down.

But if the roller coaster is built correctly, the car will make it to the top, and then gravity will take over again and the ride will continue!

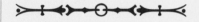

The Inventor's Times

SEPTEMBER 13, 1888   VOLUME XXXVIII No. 37   PRICE: ONE CENT

MOTORCAR BECOMES OVERNIGHT SUCCESS

Inventor's Wife Drives 65 Miles to Boost Business

MANNHEIM, GERMANY – When Karl Benz began selling the first gasoline-fueled motorcar earlier this year, business was slow. Most people believed that motorcars were unreliable and dangerous. Some even believed they were powered by evil forces.

But all of that changed last month—and now business is booming!

Everyone agrees that Mr. Benz's wife, Bertha, is responsible for the amazing turnaround. Bertha was frustrated because no one appreciated the incredible potential of her husband's motorcar—so she decided to prove its usefulness

Karl and Bertha Benz

by driving her two children from Mannheim to Pforzheim, a city 65 miles (104km) away.

"I told the boys, 'Go get in your father's motor car.' And then off we went," she explained. This is easily the longest distance ever traveled by motorcar, and the trip lasted most of the day. At one point, the car hit speeds of seven miles (eleven km) per hour!

Out for a drive: Bertha Benz and her sons arrive in Pforzheim.

The citizens of Pforzheim were stunned by her arrival. "I can't believe a woman traveled such a great distance in such a powerful machine!" exclaimed Gisela Ingall, a local seam-

(continued on page 2)

WE ASKED OUR READERS

It appears that the motorcar is here to stay. We asked the citizens of Mannheim where they wanted to go tomorrow.

28% The Blacksmith's
32% The Butcher's
20% The Strudel Shop
15% Heinrich, the light bulb maker's shop
5% Outer space

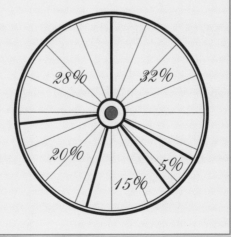

IN THIS WEEK'S NEWS

George Eastman Patents "Kodak" Camera

New "Revolving Door" Is a Dizzying Experience

Invention of Adding Machine Makes Cents for Accountants

HOW IT WORKS

WITH PROFESSOR
JIMINY G. SNOOF

Motorcars are powered by internal combustion engines. This may sound like a mouthful, but if you can understand how a cannon fires a cannonball, you can understand how this engine operates. Cannons and engines both use controlled explosions to generate power.

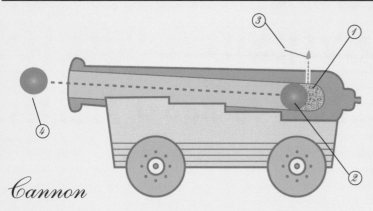

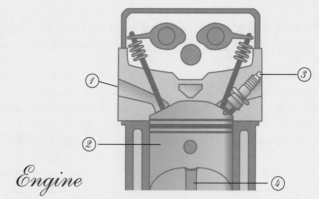

Cannon

① BEFORE THE CANNONBALL IS IN THE CANNON, GUNPOWDER IS ADDED.

② THE CANNONBALL IS LOADED, PACKING IN THE GUNPOWDER.

③ THE FUSE IS LIT, AND THIS IGNITES THE GUNPOWDER.

④ THE CANNONBALL IS FORCED FROM THE CANNON, AND THE SMOKE FROM THE GUNPOWDER ESCAPES.

Engine

① FUEL AND AIR ENTER ONE OF THE ENGINE'S CHAMBERS.

② THE PISTON PUSHES INTO THE CHAMBER AND INCREASES THE PRESSURE ON THE FUEL AND AIR.

③ A SPARK IGNITES THE FUEL.

④ THE PISTON IS PUSHED OUT OF THE CHAMBER AND THE EXHAUST ESCAPES. THIS PISTON POWERS THE ENGINE.

(continued from page 1)

stress. "And she even brought her children!"

All of the publicity and attention has been great for business, but Mrs. Benz downplays her part in the motorcar's sudden success. "Karl builds good, useful automobiles," she told us. "Sometimes people just need to see something before they can believe it."

DID YOU KNOW?

with Guest Expert Otto Mohbiel

The idea of replacing horse and carriage with a motorized vehicle is not a new one. Possibly the earliest attempt was the Fardier, a three-wheeled machine built by French engineer Nicolas Joseph Cugnot in 1771. Cugnot's attempt was powered by steam and chugged along at 2.3 miles (3.7km) per hour. In addition to being slower than a horse-drawn wagon, it was more difficult to drive. It's no surprise the Fardier didn't catch on! ●

FOUR WHEELS GOOD, THREE WHEELS BAD

AN EDITORIAL
BY FARMER
GUSTAV SCHICK

If you ask me, I think the new Benz motorcar is overrated. The biggest problem is the car's three-wheel design. It makes driving impossible. All of the roads in my village have two deep ruts that have been worn away from wagon traffic. As a result, the front wheel of my motorcar rides on the uneven ground between these ruts, and it's a very bumpy journey. I think a smart inventor would get to work on a four-wheel motorcar, with wheels just like a wagon. As soon as they're available, I'm going to buy one.

VERBAL T. TAYLOR TELLS YOU

WHAT'S IN A NAME

AUTO + MOBILE = AUTOMOBILE

AUTO is from the Greek *autós*, which means "self"

MOBILE is from the Latin *mobilis*, which means "moveable"

The Inventor's Times

DECEMBER 29, 1895   **VOLUME XVL NO. 52**   **PRICE: TWO CENTS**

X-RAY VISION DISCOVERED!

Wilhelm C. Roentgen Photographs the Inside of His Wife's Hand

Roentgen (above) and the first X-ray photograph (right).

"You Can See the Bones!!!"

WURZBERG GERMANY – Yesterday afternoon, physicist Wilhelm C. Roentgen stunned the medical community when he showed scientists the inside of his wife's hand. Amazingly, no surgical procedure was necessary—Roentgen produced an image of the hand with the use of a new technology called X-radi-ation (X-rays, for short).

Roentgen has named his finding X-rays because even he is not sure what he has found ("X" is a scientific symbol for the unknown). His discovery began last month, while he was conducting an experiment in his laboratory with a tube containing electricity. It was very dark and Mr. Roentgen noticed that some equipment on his workstation had mysteriously started to glow. Roentgen continued to experiment and discovered that the object was glowing because of invisible rays coming from the tube.

Roentgen told a friend, "I have discovered something interesting, but I do not know whether or not my observations are correct."

Additional research showed that the rays inside the tube could be used with film, like a camera, to "photograph" the inside of the body. This incredible machine has earned the support of the great

(continued on page 2)

IN THIS WEEK'S NEWS

New Sport Called Football Being Played in U.S.

Everyone's reading H. G. Wells's *The Time Machine*

Winner of First U.S. Auto Race Goes 10 MPH!

WE ASKED OUR READERS

What would you use an X-ray machine for?

Franz Holst, Dentist, 43: "It's pretty hard to see the teeth at the back of the mouth. But these X-ray machines could give me the perfect view!"

Sven Svortsen, Railroad Security Guard, 21: "I'd like to use X-rays to peek inside a passenger's luggage. You know, to make sure he's not carrying any dangerous weapons."

Gretal Defoe, Schoolgirl, 8: "Once I was helping my sister and I swallowed a button. She was very mad and she said the button would stay in my stomach for nine months and then it would grow into a sweater. Is that true?"

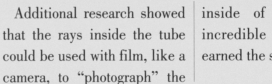

DO YOU HAVE X-RAY VISION?

We here at *The Inventor's Times* have managed to secure an X-ray machine for our own use. We've used it to photograph six different animals. Can you identify these creatures?

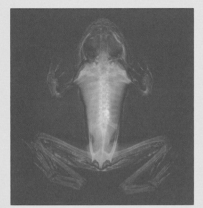
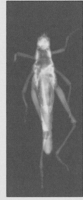
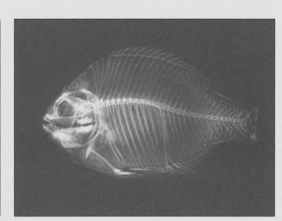
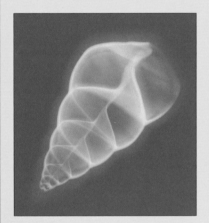
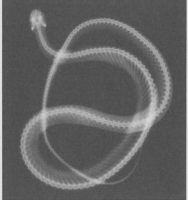

Answers (clockwise from top left):
frog, grasshopper, fish, seahorse, snake, snail.

(continued from page 1)

Thomas Edison, who believes that some day all people will have an X-ray machine in their homes. With such a device, Mr. Edison believes people will take X-ray photographs of themselves and send the images to their doctors for proper diagnosis.

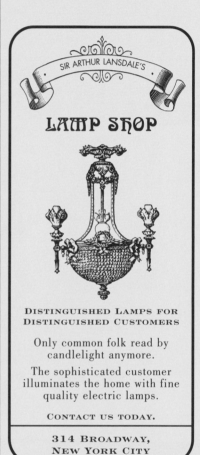
HOW IT WORKS

WITH PROFESSOR JIMINY G. SNOOF

An X-ray machine works like a camera—but it uses X-rays instead of visible light to expose the film. Since bones, fat, and muscle absorb X-rays at different levels, the image on the film will give you a clear picture of the different structures of the body. The more solid an object, the more likely it is to absorb the X-rays, which causes a shadow to be produced on the film. It is thought that X-rays will allow an "inside view" into almost anything!

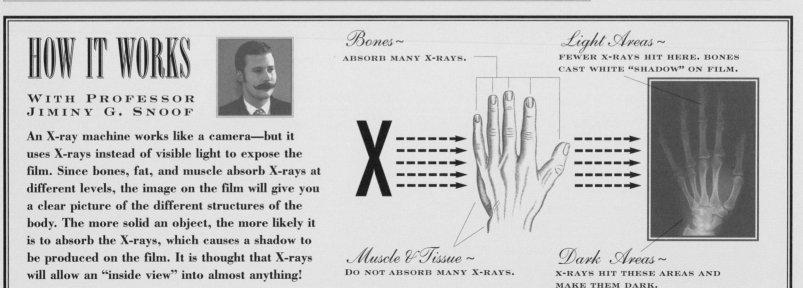

Bones~ ABSORB MANY X-RAYS.

Light Areas~ FEWER X-RAYS HIT HERE. BONES CAST WHITE "SHADOW" ON FILM.

Muscle & Tissue ~ DO NOT ABSORB MANY X-RAYS.

Dark Areas~ X-RAYS HIT THESE AREAS AND MAKE THEM DARK.

The Inventor's Times

NOVEMBER 28, 1900   VOLUME L NO. 48   PRICE: TWO CENTS

ESCALATOR TAKES 1st PRIZE AT WORLD'S FAIR

Judges Proclaim "One Small Step for Man, One Giant Ride for Mankind"

PARIS, FRANCE – More than 50 million people attended this year's World's Fair to learn about the future of the twentieth century. Among the crowd were hundreds of inventors, many of whom were showcasing their latest creations, all eager to win the competition for best invention. But the person walking away with the First Prize is Charles D. Seeberger, the inventor of the escalator.

"It's like a regular staircase, only much better," says Monsieur Jacques Perrier, a spectator who took a ride on the new machine. "The stairs do all the walking for you." But this

Attendee Jacques Perrier

award has generated a lot of controversy. Some inventors insist that Jesse Reno's "Inclined Elevator," also showcased at the World's Fair, is a far superior escalator. The Inclined Elevator resembles a long conveyor belt that slopes uphill. It debuted as an amusement ride at Coney Island, and features an important safety feature that prevents shoelaces from getting caught.

But Seeberger's invention won the hearts of the judges, mostly because of its endless series of steps, which appear

Paris was home to this year's World's Fair.

to "grow" at the bottom and "disappear" at the top. In a confidential interview with *The Inventor's Times*, one judge told us, "Now we've all

(continued on page 2)

VERBAL T. TAYLOR TELLS YOU

WHAT'S IN A NAME

SCALA + ELEVATOR = ESCALATOR

Scala is the Latin word for "steps."

IN THIS WEEK'S NEWS

Norwegian Johaan Vaaler Invents Paper Clip!

Sigmund Freud Says Dreams Are "Map to Unconscious"

Clementines Are Popular New Fruit in France

HOW IT WORKS

WITH PROFESSOR
JIMINY G. SNOOF

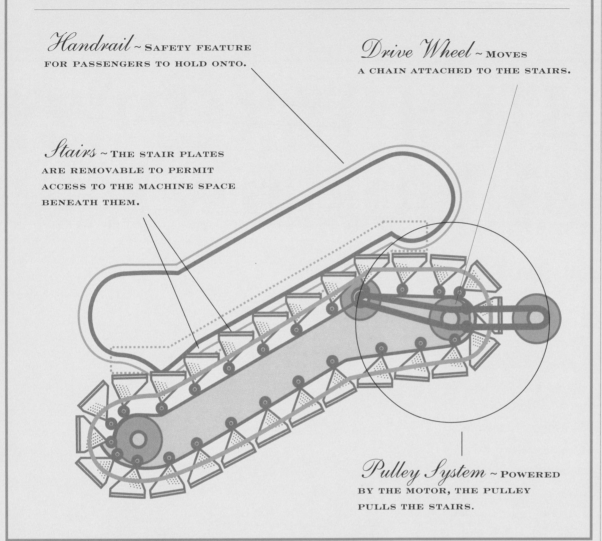

Handrail ~ SAFETY FEATURE
FOR PASSENGERS TO HOLD ONTO.

Drive Wheel ~ MOVES
A CHAIN ATTACHED TO THE STAIRS.

Stairs ~ THE STAIR PLATES
ARE REMOVABLE TO PERMIT
ACCESS TO THE MACHINE SPACE
BENEATH THEM.

Pulley System ~ POWERED
BY THE MOTOR, THE PULLEY
PULLS THE STAIRS.

HOW THE ESCALATOR MEASURES UP

	ESCALATOR	LADDER	ELEVATOR	STAIRS	SUPER SPRING JUMPING SHOES
CAN REACH A SECOND STORY WINDOW	No	Yes	No	No	Yes
ONE-STEP TRAVEL	Yes	No	Yes	No	No
EASY TO FALL OFF	No	Yes	No	No	Yes
CAN GET STUCK ON	Yes—so tie your shoelaces!	Only if you're afraid of heights!	Yes	No	No

(continued from page 1)

seen the future of climbing stairs. This is truly one small step for man, one giant ride for mankind."

Adults aren't the only ones who love the new escalator. Kids at the World's Fair are constantly trying to walk up a "down" escalator, or down an "up" escalator. City Police Inspector Pierre Gaston says, "Those crazy kids better stay off this incredible new invention, or I'm going to call their parents!"

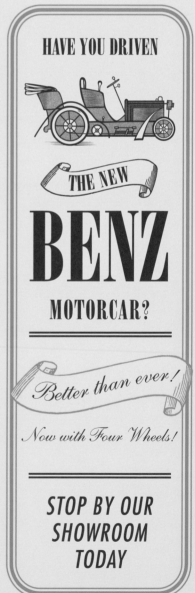

The Inventor's Times

SEPTEMBER 18, 1903   VOLUME LIII NO. 38   PRICE: TWO CENTS

COOL KIDS CRAVE CRAYOLA CRAYONS!

Nerds Continue to Use Pencils, Chalk

EASTON, PENNSYLVANIA – Until recently, Edwin Binney and C. Harold Smith's most famous invention was Au-Du-Septic, a new kind of "dust-less" chalk for teachers in classrooms. Big deal, right? But now Binney and Smith have created a new kind of crayon designed just for kids— and these crazy Crayolas are sweeping the nation.

Unlike the oily, greasy crayons you may be familiar with, Crayola crayons do not leave a sticky residue on your hands, clothes, and desk. Plus, they come in eight great colors: red, orange, yellow, green, blue, violet, brown, and black. That's a deal for five cents!

For several years now, Binney & Smith Co. has been manufacturing thick black crayons for use in factories, where people would use them to write on boxes. These crayons are made from paraffin wax, which is similar to candle wax (and very different from ear wax).

One day, a Binney & Smith salesman noticed that kids didn't have anything good to draw with. So the company added some coloring to the paraffin wax, and made the crayons small enough to fit in a child's hand.

Inventors Edwin Binney (left) and C. Harold Smith (right).

Crayola crayons have been a huge success, and kids all over the country love drawing with them. Here in Easton, the most popular kid in school is now Jessica Swizzleheart, who has eight boxes of Crayola crayons—that's 64 crayons in all! The second most popular kid in school is Jimmy Champspurs, who has five boxes of Crayola crayons.

"That Jessica is such a spoiled brat," Champspurs

The first box of Crayola crayons.

told us. "Her daddy buys her whatever she wants."

Advisers to Jessica Swizzleheart said she was busy coloring and unavailable for comment.

Jessica Swizzleheart.

IN THIS WEEK'S NEWS:

James Kraft Starts Cheese Business

First "Tour de France" a Success

16-story "Skyscraper" Completed!

HOW ARE CRAYONS MADE?

WITH PROFESSOR JIMINY G. SNOOF

1. Workers heat the wax in a big vat. At around 100°F (40°C), the wax will begin to melt.

2. At around 200°F (82°C), workers add color pigment to the wax.

3. Workers pour the liquid wax into molds. These molds are the shape of crayons.

4. When the wax cools, the crayons will harden. Workers remove them from the molds and check them for defects. Any bad ones are thrown back in the vat, to be melted and molded again.

5. The good crayons are wrapped in their labels and shipped out!

WE ASKED OUR READERS

If you could pick the color of the next Crayola crayon, what would it be?

 Bryn Ashbourne, 9: "I want skin-colored crayons so I can draw my family, and a cat-colored crayon so I can draw my cat."

 Bobby Nester, 12: "I'd like a clear color so I can draw all over my clothes and then sneak out of class."

 Ralph Snodgrass, 6: "Why doesn't the yellow taste like lemons?"

COLOR RUBBINGS

Have you ever seen a red penny? How about a blue dime? With crayons, you can make colored rubbings of coins.

1. Take the label off your crayon.

2. Place a sheet of paper over the coin.

3. Rub the side of your crayon across the paper, over the coin.

4. Voilà! The face of the coin has been transferred—in color!—to your paper.

Here at *The Inventor's Times*, we like to use images of coins when we draw pictures. Here's what a penny would look like if Professor Snoof was on it. ➡ ➡

The Inventor's Times

DECEMBER 17, 1903   VOLUME LIII No. 51   PRICE: TWO CENTS

TWO BICYCLE MECHANICS LAUNCH INCREDIBLE FLYING MACHINE

Yes, We Said Flying Machine ! ! !

The Flyer I prepares for takeoff in Kitty Hawk, North Carolina.

WE ASKED OUR READERS

Will incredible flying machines become the transportation of tomorrow?

Abraham Borgenicht, Telephone Operator, 35: "The Wright Brothers are wasting their time. We should focus on harnessing the power of giant birds like eagles and storks. We can strap chariots to these birds and make them pull us across the sky!"

Hamilton G. Shlockfart, Unemployed, 47: "This is pure poppycock! Flying machines are another stupid fad, just like that crazy light bulb."

Susan Van Hourne, 3rd Grader, 8: "Yes, I think so. A really good flying machine could take people all the way around the world."

KITTY HAWK, NORTH CAROLINA – At 10:35 this morning, two bicycle mechanics astonished the world by making the first manned flights in a gasoline-powered flying machine.

Wilbur Wright, 36, and Orville Wright, 32, are brothers from Dayton, Ohio. They moved to Kitty Hawk three years ago with a dream of building a flying machine. The U.S. Weather Bureau told them Kitty Hawk would be an excellent place to develop the project because the town has steady winds and sandy slopes, which are ideal for rough landings.

The brothers have spent most of their lives building and repairing bicycles. They taught themselves many advanced principles of mechanics and engineering. After mastering everything there is to know about bicycles, Wilbur and Orville became obsessed with building a real, working flying machine.

They began their work by

The Wright stuff: Orville (left) and Wilbur (right).

studying the flight pattern of birds. Next, they tested their ideas by building a variety of kites. After studying the way birds and kites moved through the air, the Wright Brothers tried to duplicate these effects with their invention.

Many local residents gathered this morning to watch the launch of the flying machine, nicknamed "Flyer I." The younger brother, Orville, took

(continued on page 2)

IN THIS WEEK'S NEWS

New "Teddy" Bears are the Hot Christmas Gift

 Henry Ford Unveils New Car-Making Company

Inventor's Times Writer Verbal T. Taylor Retires

MAKE YOUR OWN PAPER FLYER

You don't need to spend three years in Kitty Hawk to build your own flyer. All it takes is a simple sheet of notebook paper. Here's how to do it:

1. Fold the paper in half lengthwise. Unfold so that the crease is "valley" side up.

2. Fold the top corners down to the center fold.

3. Fold the tip down.

4. Fold a small part of the tip up, making a crease, then unfold.

5. Fold the top corners down to the center fold, so the corners meet above the fold in the tip.

6. Fold the tip up.

7. Fold the entire plane in half, so that the tip is on the outside.

8. Fold the wings down.

(continued from page 1)

his place at the controls. After rolling for 45 feet (14m), the flying machine lifted in the air. Twelve seconds later—after traveling an additional 120 feet (36m)—the flying machine touched the ground. It really worked!

Spectators like Mildred Brockenbrower were amazed. "I was just walking along the beach," she explained. "And then I saw this giant winged machine hurtling toward me. I thought I was hallucinating!"

The Wright brothers made three additional flights today. At one point, the plane reached an amazing height of 15 feet (5m)—nearly three times the height of a person!

FLYER I SPECIFICATIONS

WINGSPAN: 40 FT 4 IN (12.3M)
LENGTH: 21 FT (6.4M)
WEIGHT: 605 LBS (274KG)
ENGINE: 12 HORSEPOWER
MAXIMUM SPEED: 30 MPH (48 KM/H)

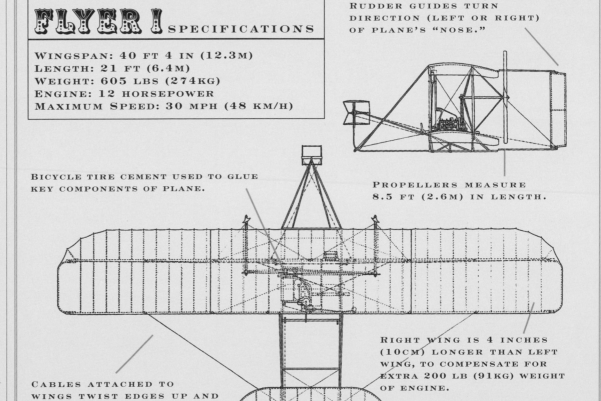

RUDDER GUIDES TURN DIRECTION (LEFT OR RIGHT) OF PLANE'S "NOSE."

PROPELLERS MEASURE 8.5 FT (2.6M) IN LENGTH.

BICYCLE TIRE CEMENT USED TO GLUE KEY COMPONENTS OF PLANE.

RIGHT WING IS 4 INCHES (10CM) LONGER THAN LEFT WING, TO COMPENSATE FOR EXTRA 200 LB (91KG) WEIGHT OF ENGINE.

CABLES ATTACHED TO WINGS TWIST EDGES UP AND DOWN, CONTROLLING ASCENSION OR DESCENT.

The Inventor's Times

FEBRUARY 7, 1906   VOLUME LVI No. 6   PRICE: THREE CENTS

NOVOCAIN MAKES DENTIST VISITS FUN!

Inventor Alfred Einhorn

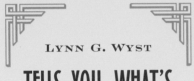

LYNN G. WYST

TELLS YOU WHAT'S IN A NAME

NOVO + CAIN = NOVOCAIN

NOVO comes from the Latin word *novus*, meaning "new."

CAIN comes from cocaine, the anesthetic drug that Novocain replaced.

"Istht like a pawty in my mowf," says patient

PHILADELPHIA, PENNSYLVANIA – Here in the City of Brotherly Love, dentists are using a new wonder drug to make their patients drool, talk funny, and feel tingly all over. The name of this drug is Novocain, and it makes painful cavity fillings a thing of the past.

"I just hab a toof pulled," says 10-year-old Ricky Figglestem. "I didn't feel a thim." Ricky's dentist gave him a shot of Novocain about five minutes before he extracted his tooth. Ricky's mouth tingled and then it went numb, but he didn't feel any pain. "I wub berry, berry, afwaid," Ricky says, "but wib da Nobocame I feel grape. Istht like a pawty in my mowf."

When your body is hurt, nerves in the injured area will send "pain signals" to your brain. Novocain is an anesthetic, which means that it temporarily puts those nerves to sleep. As a result, you don't feel any pain, and the dentist can do his job very quickly.

Up until recently, one of the only "pain killers" available to dentists was cocaine—a dangerous anesthetic with many addictive qualities. Some dentists refused to use any anesthetics, period. This explains why so many people are afraid to go to the dentist—or why so many of us have to wear false teeth.

But thanks to Novocain, which was invented by German chemist Alfred Einhorn, false

Patient Ricky Figglestem had a great time at the dentist's office.

teeth may become a thing of the past. This "wonder drug" is perfectly safe and its effects disappear after about an hour. "I am berry habby to hear dat," says Ricky Figglestem.

IN THIS WEEK'S NEWS

DUTCH LAW REQUIRES AUTO DRIVERS TO BE LICENSED

NEW *VARIETY* NEWSPAPER COVERS SHOW BUSINESS

THE INVENTOR'S TIMES WELCOMES NEW WRITER LYNN G. WYST

PAIN IS GOOD FOR YOU

An Editorial by U.S. Army Drill Sergeant Frank Faulkner

LISTEN UP, WEAKLINGS!

Pain has been getting a bad rap lately, and I think it's unfair. The truth is, we feel pain for our own PROTECTION! Let's say you're running through a training battlefield and you twist your ankle. It's going to HURT if you keep running. THAT'S BECAUSE YOUR ANKLE IS INJURED! Your body wants you to rest it! The pain is telling you, "Stop that! No more running, soldier! This ankle needs to heal!"

If you rest long enough, the pain will go away, and you'll know it's safe to start running around again. So let's give pain a break! IT'S NOT ALWAYS A BAD THING!

DID YOU KNOW

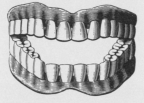

with Guest Dentist Pearl E. White

Here are some nuggets of dental trivia that I've collected over the years:

—The ancient Egyptians used tree twigs for toothbrushes. And in the 15th century, the Chinese made toothbrush bristles from the neck hairs of a Siberian wild boar.

—Men are more likely than women to suffer from chronic bad breath.

—President George Washington wore dentures made of hippopotamus teeth, walrus teeth, cow teeth, and elephant tusks.

—Right-handed people tend to chew on the right side of their mouths. Left-handed people will generally chew on the left.

—Revolutionary war hero Paul Revere ("The British are Coming! The British are Coming!") worked as a silversmith and a dentist.

THE SCIENCE OF NERVES

Here's a little demonstration to show how anesthetics work. We promise it won't hurt a bit.

MATERIALS:
Toothpicks
Ice (in a bowl)
A friend

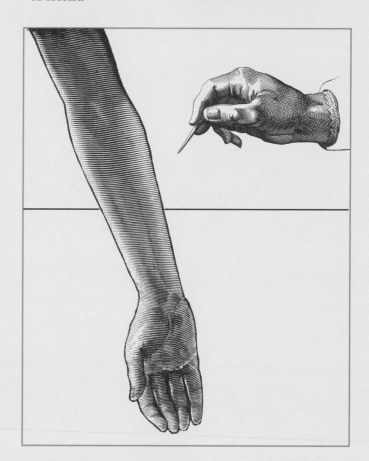

1. Close your eyes and have your friend gently press a toothpick against the inside of your forearm. Can you feel it?

2. Rub an ice cube on the inside of your forearm until the skin feels very cold.

3. Now close your eyes again and ask your friend to press the toothpick against the numbed skin. Were you more sensitive to the toothpick with the ice, or without the ice? The ice simulates the effects of anesthesia by reducing your sense of touch.

THE INVENTOR'S TIMES

NOVEMBER 19, 1913   VOLUME LXIII NO. 47   PRICE: THREE CENTS

SWINGING ARMS WIPE RAIN FROM WINDSHIELD

INVENTOR MARY ANDERSON MAKES DRIVING SAFER!

DETROIT, MICHIGAN – Most people who visit New York City remember the theaters, the museums, or Central Park. But when Mary Anderson thought about her trip to New York in 1903, her most powerful memory was of the cold and wet driver who had to wipe the snow and ice off his windshield.

This man was giving Anderson a driving tour of New York City, and she felt very sorry for him. It was raining, snowing, and sleeting, and the driver kept stopping just to clear off the slush. Many other drivers left their windows open, and leaned outside to see whenever they made a turn.

Obviously, this was very, very dangerous. And when Anderson returned home to Alabama, she couldn't stop thinking about the drivers in New York. Less than a year later, she devised a mechanism that allowed drivers of

Windshield-clearing devices are located at the top of the windshield.

motorcars to clear the windshield from inside their auto. It's very simple—the driver pulls a lever that releases a spring-loaded arm. The arm is equipped with a rubber blade, and it swings across the windshield, wiping away snow and rain.

Anderson soon applied for a patent for her windshield-clearing device. Even though she was confident about the

(continued on page 2)

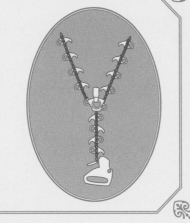

IN THIS WEEK'S NEWS

PANAMA CANAL OPENS! SAILING SHIPS EVERYWHERE

 FORD MOTOR COMPANY IS CRANKING OUT AUTOS

NEW CRACKER JACKS: THERE'S A PRIZE IN THE BOX!

(continued from page 1)

success of her invention, many of her friends were skeptical. "At the time, it seemed like just another one of Mary's crazy ideas," says Mrs. Anderson's gossipy neighbor, Esther Stufflesniff. "I told her she was wasting her time. As you can imagine, I'm the one who feels stupid now."

In 1905, Mary Anderson received a patent for the first windshield-clearing device. It has taken automobile manufacturers eight years to recognize the usefulness of this invention—but now it appears that windshield wipers will become standard with most new vehicles. The only question *The Inventor's Times* has is, What on earth took so long?

DID YOU KNOW?

with Guest Expert Ray Needay

Mary Anderson isn't the only woman who has devised improvements for the automobile. Earlier this year, silent film actress Florence Lawrence invented a "Signaling Arm" and a "Braking Indicator" so that drivers behind you will get an advance warning of your actions. The signaling arm can be raised and lowered by pressing an electric button on the automobile's dash. The arm tells other drivers which way the car is turning. The braking indicator raises a flag on the back of the automobile whenever the driver steps on the brake pedal.

Florence Lawrence

With her creation of windshield wipers, Mary Anderson has joined hundreds of other women inventors around the world. Here are just three of her fellow female tinkerers:

1870: Margaret Knight invents the flat-bottomed paper bag—the same kind that grocery stores use to this very day!

1885: Furniture store owner Sarah Goode receives a patent for a bed that folds into a cabinet. She becomes the first black woman to receive a patent in the United States.

1886: An exasperated Josephine Cochran exclaims, "If nobody else is going to invent a dishwashing machine, I'll do it myself!" Her invention is an immediate hit with restaurants and large hotels.

WE ASKED OUR READERS

Windshield Wipers, Braking Indicators, Signaling Arms—what's next? What would you like to see in an automobile?

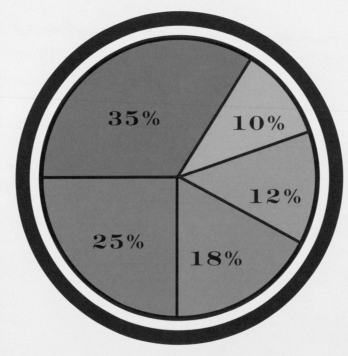

35% GIANT DICE COVERED WITH FUZZ

25% HEATING/ COOLING APPARATUS

18% VANILLA-SCENTED CHRISTMAS TREE

12% TELEPHONE

10% MEDAL OF ST. CHRISTOPHER

THE INVENTOR'S TIMES

AUGUST 15, 1921 — VOLUME LXXI NO. 33 — PRICE: FOUR CENTS

NEW BAND-AIDS ARE A WIFE SAVER!

ACCIDENT-PRONE WIFE OF INVENTOR BENEFITS FROM NEW BANDAGES

NEW YORK, NEW YORK – The first week that Earle and Josephine Dickson were married, Mrs. Dickson cut herself twice while slicing vegetables for dinner. Mr. Dickson quickly realized that his wife was accident-prone. *Very* accident-prone. Whether she was cooking dinner, cleaning her home, or completing other household chores, Mrs. Dickson couldn't seem to avoid tiny scrapes, cuts, and bruises.

Fortunately, Mr. Dickson worked for a company called

Earle and Josephine Dickson.

Johnson & Johnson, which manufactured adhesive tape and cotton gauze. One day, he cut several pieces of tape into strips, and placed a wad of gauze in the middle of each piece. Voilà! Ready-made bandages for the next time his wife injured herself.

"They're so convenient," Mrs. Dickson told *The Inventor's Times.* "You just stick them on and you're done."

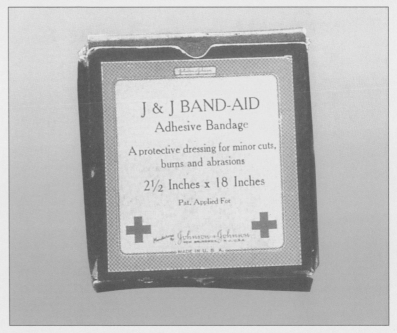

New invention is perfect for cuts, boo-boos, and owwies.

So far, these incredible bandages only have one drawback—it can really hurt to pull them off! But after researching this problem here at *The Inventor's Times*, we've determined that a few drops of baby oil can solve the problem. Just rub the oil over and under the bandage, and it should fall off in a few moments.

(continued on page 2)

COMING NEXT WEEK

ARE BAND-AIDS TOO MUCH FUN? ONE SCIENTIST EXPLAINS WHY CHILDREN MAY START HURTING THEMSELVES ON PURPOSE!

IN THIS WEEK'S NEWS

HERMANN OBERTH: "I BELIEVE WE CAN PUT ROCKETS INTO SPACE"

MED STUDENT INVENTS LIE DETECTING MACHINE

RADIO BROADCAST OF NEW YORK WORLD SERIES HEARD ALL THE WAY IN NEW JERSEY

(continued from page 1)

It wasn't long before Mr. Dickson's supervisors heard about this invention, and now Johnson & Johnson is preparing to sell this product nationwide. "They will be called Band-Aids," a spokesman announced yesterday afternoon. "You will see them on the market in the upcoming weeks. We believe that Band-Aids will help to heal wounds and protect against infection."

This news has made Mrs. Dickson quite happy. "I guess it's proof that great inventions don't need to be all big and complicated," she told our reporters while slicing carrots for a chicken soup. "Sometimes you just need a great idea and—whoops! Look what I've done. Cut myself again. Can you pass me one of those Band-Aids?"

How to Treat a Scraped Knee

EXPERT ADVICE
BY NURSE MARY SHEEPSHANKS

Next time your friend scrapes his or her knee, there are a few simple steps you can take to stop the bleeding. First, ask your friend to lie down and elevate the leg (you can do this by placing the leg up on a couch or chair).

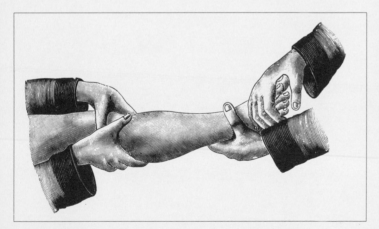

Next, place some clean bandages on the cut and apply pressure. If you don't have bandages, try clean paper towels. This will help the blood to clot. Finally, go find an adult who can take a look at the wound, and decide if your friend needs to see a doctor.

DID YOU KNOW?

with Guest Expert Mynnie Hertz

In case of an emergency, always remain calm, call for help, and find an adult immediately.

Run minor burns under cold water immediately after they happen. It will reduce the pain.

If your clothes or someone else's clothes catch fire, don't run. Stop, drop, and roll until the flames go out. Then call for help.

Wash out minor cuts with soap and water, then cover them with a bandage.

If someone is hit on the head and is unconscious, call for help. Never move the head or neck. Stay calm, and wait for emergency help to arrive. Do not leave the person alone. Don't allow anyone to move the person until help arrives.

Create an Emergency Action Plan

Every home should have an emergency action plan. Using a pencil and a sheet of paper, copy this information, and ask an adult to help you fill in the blanks. Then keep it on your refrigerator for easy reference.

MY EMERGENCY ACTION PLAN

In case of emergency, I should dial:_____

My neighbor _____
can be reached at: _____

My relative_____
can be reached at: _____

My street address is:

_____

_____

The cross street is:

_____

My phone number is:_____

REMEMBER: NEVER HANG UP UNTIL THE OPERATOR TELLS YOU TO!

THE INVENTOR'S TIMES

SEPTEMBER 25, 1923   VOLUME LXXIII NO. 39   PRICE: FOUR CENTS

"SEPARABLE FASTENER" RECEIVES ZIPPIER NAME

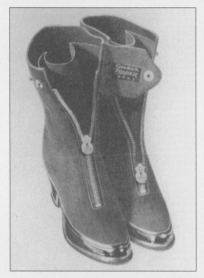 

New "Zipper" Boots (left); Whitcomb Judson (right)

"ZIPPER" IS BIG HIT WITH FASHION DESIGNERS EVERYWHERE

HOBOKEN, NEW JERSEY – To understand why everyone is talking about zippers, we need to think back to 1893 and inventor Whitcomb Judson, who had a friend with a bad back. Whenever this friend leaned over to lace up his boots, his back just felt worse, so Whitcomb designed an early version of the zipper which he patented as a "Clasp-Locker." It jammed often and didn't stay closed too well—but it was successful enough for Whitcomb to start his own business, the Universal Fastener Company (UFC).

Executives at the UFC realized that Clasp-Lockers would need a zippier name, so they marketed them as "Judson C-Curity Fasteners." In 1917 UFC engineer Gideon Sunbach re-designed the product and changed the name to "Separable Fasteners." The U.S. Army liked the new version of the product and placed large orders for uniforms and gear. But the general public was still using

(continued on page 2)

IN THIS WEEK'S NEWS

NEW "WINDOW POLISH" CLEANS BETTER THAN WATER!

CLARENCE BIRDSEYE PLANS RELEASE OF "FROZEN FOOD"

GERMANY UNVEILS GEOCENTRIC "PLANETARIUM"

NAME THAT INVENTION

If all inventions began with lousy names like Judson's C-Curity Fasteners, you might have seen the eight products listed below. Can you guess what the real names are?

1. Tom's Illuminated Electro Sphere
2. Swinging Hydro-Wiping Auto Arms
3. Long Distance Voice Transporting Box
4. Inky Letter-Stamping Paper Press
5. Mechanically Powered Rolling Transport
6. Einhorn's Numb and Tingly Mouth Juice
7. See-Through Bone-Vision Camera
8. Gravity-Induced Fun Cart

(Answers: 1. Light Bulb 2. Windshield Wipers 3. Telephone 4. Typewriter 5. Automobile 6. Novocain 7. X-Rays 8. Rollercoaster)

(continued from page 1)

buttons and laces.

Meanwhile, in Akron, Ohio, inventor B. F. Goodrich (who had started his own rubber company) was busy designing a pair of rubber shoes called "galoshes." He thought that Separable Fasteners would be perfect for his shoes, but he decided that the invention needed a zippier name—something like, well, zipper!

The newly named invention has electrified the fashion industry. "These cute little zippers are extraordinary!" shrieked fashion designer Sterling Ambrosia. "I simply must have one hundred of them, and I'll need them by tomorrow, darling. My clients are waiting."

U.S. Army Drill Sergeant Frank Faulkner also enjoys the zippers. "A good soldier doesn't have time for buttons or laces, sir!" he shouted to reporters earlier this morning. "A good solider needs to shut up, zip up, and ship out!"

Sergeant Frank Faulkner

One lesson is definitely clear: if you're going to invent something, make sure you create a zippy name for it!

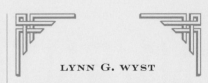

LYNN G. WYST

TELLS YOU WHAT'S IN A NAME

B. F. Goodrich chose the name zipper because it was **onomatopoetic** (on-oh-mott-uh-poh-eh-tic). This is just a fancy way of saying that the sound of the word describes a sound, like boom, buzz, or slurp. ZIP is the sound that a fastener makes when it is opened or closed.

HISTORY OF THE "Zipper"

1893

Whitcomb Judson makes the "Clasp Locker," also known as the "C-Curity Fastener."

1917

Gideon Sundbach updates design, calls it "Separable Fastener."

1923

B. F. Goodrich adds to rubber boots, calls it the "Zipper."

A PEEK INSIDE THE ZIPPER

TOP STOPS
These prevent you from pulling the slider off track.

PULL-TAB

TEETH
When these teeth pass through the slider, they are linked or separated.

SLIDER BODY
The slider joins or separates the teeth of the zipper.

BOTTOM STOP
This prevents you from pulling the slider off track.

THE INVENTOR'S TIMES

SEPTEMBER 21, 1928   VOLUME LXXVII, NO. 39   PRICE: FOUR CENTS

INVENTOR HAS NO TRUBBLE MAKING DUBBLE BUBBLE

BUBBLE BLOWERS POPPING UP EVERYWHERE

PHILADELPHIA, PENNSYLVANIA – Walter Diemer is an accountant for the Fleer Chewing Gum Company. He is supposed to add and subtract numbers, not experiment with gum recipes. But for a long time now, Mr. Diemer has been trying to perfect a recipe for something he calls "bubble gum."

Yesterday morning, his dream finally came true. After many failed experiments, Mr. Diemer created a batch of gum that stretches easily and isn't as sticky as regular chewing gum—so you can peel it off your face after the bubble pops!

To test the product, Mr. Diemer brought a five-pound

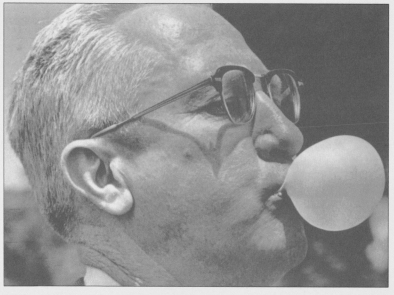

Walter Diemer demonstrates his bubble blowing technique.

block of the new bubble gum to his local grocery store. The product sold out almost instantly. "We were shocked," said grocer Emily Walters. "I thought he'd sell four or five pieces at the most. But five pounds? Holy moley!"

For thousands of years, people all over the world—including the ancient Greeks and Mayans—have been chewing gum. The earliest gum came from the sap of trees. In recent years, manufacturers have started to add sugar, softeners, corn syrup,

and flavors to gum.

Mr. Diemer calls his new gum Dubble Bubble, and the

(continued on page 2)

IN THIS WEEK'S NEWS

AMELIA EARHART IS FIRST WOMAN TO FLY ACROSS THE ATLANTIC

GERMANY INTRODUCES HOT-AIR HAND DRYING APPARATUS

WOODBRIDGE, NEW JERSEY IS HOME TO FIRST CLOVERLEAF INTERSECTION

We Asked Our Readers

What impact will bubble gum have on your life?

Edna Whipper, School Teacher, 74: "If I see one of these bubbles in my classroom, there will be a severe price to pay! And I'm not talking about detention, either!"

Emily Walters, Grocer, 38: "I love it! If I sell just 99,999,912 more pieces, I'll be a millionaire!"

Harold D'Angelo, Sanitation Worker, 40: "If it's less sticky than regular gum, I'll love it. I hate scraping gum off the street."

(continued from page 1)

Fleer Chewing Gum Company is already planning to mass-produce this fancy new gum for a penny a piece. Mr. Diemer is incredibly proud of his success. "I've done something with my life," he told reporters yesterday. "I've made kids happy around the world."

?????????????????????????

DID YOU KNOW?

?????????????????????????

**with Guest Expert
Bubba Blour, D.D.S.**

- Swallowed bubble gum will not get stuck in your intestines, but it will pass through your system in one piece, because gum base cannot be digested.
- Many doctors say chewing gum helps people quit smoking. After all, if you had a great stick of gum in your mouth, why would you want a cigarette?
- The U.S. military issues gum to soldiers because it helps people concentrate on their work and boosts morale.
- Detectives can identify criminals by comparing the suspect's chewed gum to his dental records.

?????????????????????????

HOW TO BLOW A BUBBLE INSIDE A BUBBLE

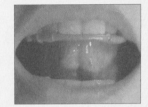

1. Chew a big fat piece of gum, or chew two small pieces together.

2. Using your tongue and the roof of your mouth, flatten the gum.

3. Use your tongue to press the gum against the back of your teeth.

4. Open your teeth a little bit and push the center of the gum through the opening.

5. Pull back your tongue. Now blow a bubble!

6. Here's the tricky part: To blow a bubble inside the bubble, repeat steps 2 through 5 while your first bubble is still inflated. It will take some practice!

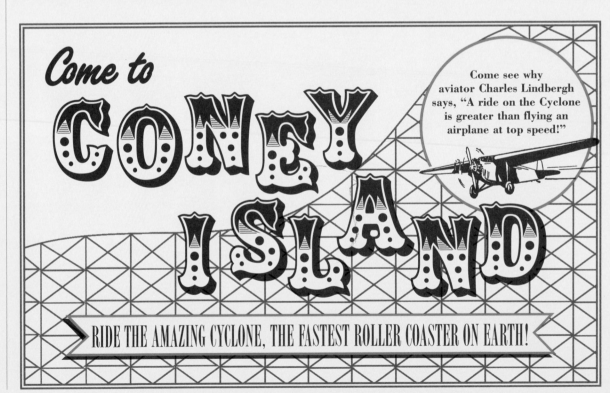

THE INVENTOR'S TIMES

NOVEMBER 19, 1928   VOLUME LXXVIII NO. 47   PRICE: FIVE CENTS

EEK! DISNEY MAKES ANIMATION HISTORY

SYNCHRONIZED SOUND AND A MOUSE NAMED MICKEY

NEW YORK, NEW YORK – Last night, people in the Colony Theatre laughed and cheered as a mouse tried to impress his girlfriend. Now if you think a pair of lovesick rodents invaded the concession stand, think again. The audience was actually watching Walt Disney's *Steamboat Willie*, the first animated cartoon with synchronized sound.

Until now, cartoons were projected on a screen while a person in the theater—usually a piano player—performed live music. But after Walt Disney saw *The Jazz Singer*, the first motion picture with synchronized sound, he felt that cartoons should have sound, too.

Walt Disney and his friend Ub Iwerks, an illustrator, had already made two silent cartoons featuring the star of *Steamboat Willie*, Mickey Mouse, but no theaters wanted to show them. But Disney refused to give up on his cartoon hero.

In *Steamboat Willie*, Mickey rescues his girlfriend, Minnie, from a dreadful steamboat captain named Pete. As Mickey runs away from the pirate, he uses the animals on board to play the song "Turkey in the Straw." He taps on a cow's teeth like a xylophone.

(continued on page 2)

Steamboat Willie has made Mickey Mouse a star.

© Disney Enterprises, Inc.

© Disney Enterprises, Inc.

Inventor Walt Disney.

IN THIS WEEK'S NEWS

ALEXANDER FLEMING MAKES IT BIG WITH PENICILLIN

JACOB SCHICK PATENTS FIRST ELECTRIC RAZOR

VITAMIN C ISOLATED FROM CITRUS FRUITS

LYNN G. WYST

TELLS YOU —➤ WHAT'S IN A NAME

ANIMATE comes from the Latin word *animatus,* and it means "filled with breath or air." To animate something is to give life to it.

(continued from page 1)

He also makes some piglets squeal along to the music.

Audiences were thrilled. "That mouse was hilarious," exclaimed Mel Kittage, a high school senior from Brooklyn. "What I wouldn't give to have his face on a T-shirt."

The management of the Colony Theatre also thinks that Walt Disney is on to something, and they've guaranteed Disney $500 a week if they can continue to show *Steamboat Willie* at the theater. "You mark my words," usher Vinnie Panzarella told us, while counting the money from the evening's performance. "Dat little mouse is gonna be a big star."

?????????????????????????

DID YOU KNOW?

?????????????????????????

**With Guest Expert
Anne Emmett**

Mickey Mouse was almost Mortimer Mouse. Walt Disney came up with the idea for his mouse on a train from New York to Los Angeles, and named him Mortimer. His wife thought that Mickey sounded better. Disney thought so, too, and by the time they arrived in Los Angeles, he had changed the name to Mickey Mouse.

?????????????????????????

How Does It Work?

**With Professor
Jiminy Snoof, Jr.**

When we watch animated cartoons, we're really watching a series of still images. These images are shown very quickly—at a speed of 24 images per second—so our eyes and brains are tricked into seeing a single image that appears to be moving.

To make a movie, cartoonists draw lots and lots of pictures. Each one is just slightly different than the last: Though *Steamboat Willie* is only seven minutes long, the film contains more than 10,000 images—all drawn by hand!

Make Your Own Animated Cartoon

It's easy to do simple animation—and you don't need to draw 10,000 images to get started!

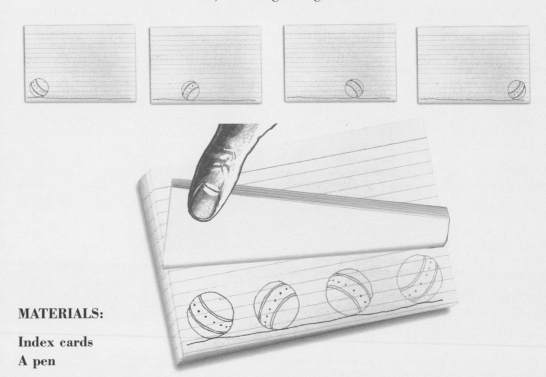

MATERIALS:

**Index cards
A pen**

1. Make sure your index cards are in a neat pile. On the top index card, draw a ball in the bottom left corner.

2. On the next card, draw the same ball, but place it slightly to the right of the first ball. If your ball has a pattern, adjust it so the ball appears to be rolling. Repeat this step on additional cards until the ball has reached the bottom right corner.

3. While keeping the cards in a neat pile, flip through them with your thumb. Watch the ball roll across the bottom!

4. Now turn the cards upside-down and start over. This time, can you make the ball bounce? Can you try animating a car? How about a bird?

THE ☀ INVENTOR'S TIMES

APRIL 30, 1939   VOLUME LXXXIX NO. 18   PRICE: SIX CENTS

"MUST SEE" TV IS WORLD'S FAIR HIGHLIGHT

President's Speech Is "Televised" Across the City

Live from New York! It's the President!

The first television.

NEW YORK, NEW YORK – "Those who come to the World's Fair will find that the eyes of America are fixed on the future." With these words, President Franklin D. Roosevelt welcomed visitors to the start of yesterday's World's Fair. But as the President spoke, people all over New York were watching him, thanks to a new invention called the television, or TV for short.

Ninth-grader George Skitori

saw the President in his cousin Eddie's living room. Baker Angela Simms saw the President while working at the Park Avenue Sweet Shoppe. And stockbroker Martin Scrimshaw saw the President in the lobby of the Empire State Building.

Television allows the image of the President to appear in all of these places at the same time. The World's Fair used special cameras to capture the image and sound of the

President's speech. These cameras delivered the information to the Empire State Building. From there, the speech was broadcast across the city. Anyone who owned a television receiver could "tune in" the event.

"Not many people own televisions right now," explained World's Fair attendee David Kearn, "because no one is making television programs. But I think that's going to change very soon."

Kearn is absolutely right. The radio company RCA used the World's Fair to announce that they are starting a new division of their company that

(continued on page 2)

LYNN G. WYST

TELLS YOU
WHAT'S IN A NAME

TELE + VISION = TELEVISION

TELE is a Greek word meaning "distant" or "from afar."

VISION means "sight" or "the act of sensing with the eyes."

IN THIS WEEK'S NEWS

New "Instant Coffee" trademarked "Nescafé"

Marjorie Kinnan Rawlings wins Pulitzer Prize for *The Yearling*

U.S. government now offering "Food Stamps"

THE FUTURE OF TELEVISION

An Editorial by Psychic Gypsy Magda Pantazopolous

Future very cloudy, sorry, Magda cannot see. Wait—no—future clearer now. Magda sees potatoes. Little potato families. Sitting on couches. Where do potatoes come from? Magda cannot say. Potatoes do not see Magda. They shake wands at screen and picture changes. Picture shows survivors on island. The island people are very angry. They send outcast away from village. Outcast is very sad, very sad. Potatoes are very sad. But potatoes shake wand and picture changes again. Now more survivors on new island. Magda see Professor and Movie Star. Magda see silly man in red shirt. Silly man is hit by coconut. Potatoes very happy now. Potatoes laugh and laugh and laugh.

TELEVISION INVENTORS

FARNSWORTH

— VERSUS —

ZWORYKIN

If you ask the question, "Who invented the television?" you're likely to receive two different answers: Vladimer Zworykin or Philo T. Farnsworth. Here's why:

Farnsworth successfully broadcast the first television image on September 7, 1927. The image of a dollar sign was displayed on a screen that was 1¼ inches (4cm) square. It was a little blurry, but the transmission was a success.

Zworykin submitted an application to the U.S. Patent Office in 1923 for an "Iconoscope," a device that he used to transmit an image. But Zworykin didn't demonstrate a successful transmission until 1934.

Some tell us that Zworykin's design didn't work, and he was only successful after he visited Farnsworth's lab. Others feel that Zworykin developed television first, and Farnsworth played an important role in improving Zworykin's innovations.

(continued from page 1)

will specialize in television programs. The new company will be known as the National Broadcasting Company, or NBC for short. NBC plans to transmit films, fashion shows, operas, and even sporting events throughout the year.

In another demonstration of the television, RCA President David Sarnoff looked into the camera and told his audience, "Now we add radio sight to sound!"

HOW IT WORKS

With Professor Jiminy Snoof, Jr.

A televised image is based on a very simple principle: if you divide a picture into a series of very tiny colored dots, your brain will view the dots as a meaningful image.

If the dots are too big, they will look meaningless. Take this photograph of me, for example:

This picture looks blurry and unfocused. But if you stand back ten feet from this paper, the dots will become small enough for your brain to "see" my beautiful face.

Your television screen has hundreds of small dots (if you put your face against the screen, you'll be able to see them). The result is a clear picture that changes at least 24 times per second, to present the illusion of motion. (For further information, see our feature story on the animated cartoon from September 18, 1924.)

THE INVENTOR'S TIMES

MARCH 6, 1943   VOLUME XCIII NO. 10   PRICE: SIX CENTS

COPYING MACHINE STILL IN LIMBO LIMBO LIMBO LIMBO

20 Companies Reject Inventor's Idea for Copying Documents

ASTORIA, NEW YORK – Five years have passed since Chester Carlson made the first photocopy of a document, but he still can't convince people that his invention is worthwhile. IBM, General Electric, RCA, and Kodak have all passed on a chance to be the exclusive manufacturers of Carlson's "copying machine."

"We listened to what he had to say," said William Danforth, president of the Ceres Corporation. "We just didn't think it was a very good idea. If I need a copy, I just holler for my secretary."

Carlson came up with the idea for his invention while working for a company that often submitted paperwork to the U.S. patent office. Carlson had to make multiple copies of patents by hand, which can take several hours. Plus, Carlson has poor eyesight and arthritis. He decided there was a need for a machine that, in his words, "could be right in an office where you could bring a document to it, push it in a slot, and get a copy out."

To research his idea, Carlson spent many months at the New York Public Library and read hundreds of scientific articles. Then he hired an unemployed German physicist named Otto Kornei to help him with his experiments. They were able to create a copy of a slide that read

(continued on page 2)

Inventor Chester Carlson.

The first photocopy of a document.

COMING NEXT WEEK

What are contact lenses and how will they work? *The Inventor's Times* has all of the early predictions.

IN THIS WEEK'S NEWS

U.S. Teens Dancing the Jitterbug, Parents Disapprove

Teflon No-Stick Surface—Great for Military, Eggs

Jackson Pollock Splatters Paint on Canvas; Critics Call It Art

(continued from page 1)

"10-22-38 Astoria," which was the date and place of their experiment. Carlson and Kornei were amazed by their success and went out to lunch to celebrate.

Since then, there has been very little to cheer about. The repeated rejections have left Carlson feeling pretty lousy. However, the inventor still believes in his copying machine, and we're encouraging him to stick with it. Sooner or later, this amazing machine has to catch on!

HOW IT WORKS

With Professor Jiminy Snoof, Jr.

OPPOSITE CHARGES ATTRACT

SIMILAR CHARGES REPEL

Chester Carlson's photocopy machine works its magic thanks to a fine black powder called "toner" and the magic of static electricity. But before I can explain how static electricity is created, you need to understand three things:

1. Everything in our world is composed of atoms.
2. Atoms are composed of protons (positive-charged particles), electrons (negative-charged particles), and neutrons (uncharged particles).
3. Opposites attract—especially with atoms! A positive-charged proton will always be attracted to a negative-charged electron, and vice versa.

Most atoms have the same number of protons and electrons, so the positive and negative charges balance themselves out—the result is no charge.

But when you rub two items together, electrons can "jump" from atom to atom, creating an imbalance. Electrons could jump from the carpet to your sneakers, or from your hand to a metal doorknob. They'll do this because they're attracted to protons in other atoms. And whenever this happens, static electricity is created. To test it out, try the balloon experiment on this page.

WE ASKED OUR READERS

If Carlson's invention ever gets off the ground, what will you be copying?

Joey Ratface, Ninth Grader, 14: "I would copy some geek's homework so that I didn't have to do it myself."

Melissa Goode, Eighth Grader, 13: "I'd make a new copy of the Declaration of Independence, because the original is getting pretty old. I think it would be in our nation's interest to have a nice, clean copy on good paper."

Freddy Garbanzo, Independent Contractor, 44: "I got a hundred dollar bill I'd love to copy. You get me in a room with this fella, maybe the three of us can start our own little business. Off the books, you know?"

STATIC ELECTRICITY IN ACTION

MATERIALS
   1 round balloon
   1 mirror

WHAT TO DO:
1. Inflate the balloon and knot it.
2. Rub the balloon on your hair for about 15 seconds. Be sure to rub around the whole balloon. Now look in the mirror. What has happened to your hair?
3. What happens when you bring the balloon close to your hair? Or when you pull it away?

WHY IT WORKS:
When you rubbed the balloon on your hair, electrons transferred from your head to the balloon, giving it a negative charge. All of your hairs were left with a positive charge. And since only opposite charges attract, each of your hairs is standing straight up, to get away from all the others! When you bring the balloon back to your head, your hair is attracted to it, because the balloon has a negative charge and your hair has a positive charge.

THE INVENTOR'S TIMES

OCTOBER 30, 1945 — VOLUME XCV NO. 44 — PRICE: SIX CENTS

AMAZING NEW PEN MAKES POINT ABOUT PATENTS

Department Store Sells 10,000 Pens For $12.50 Each!

Gimbel's customers are bonkers for ballpoints!

NEW YORK, NEW YORK – More than 5,000 people gathered outside of Gimbel's Department Store yesterday with the hope of purchasing a new Reynolds Rocket ballpoint pen.

"I've already thrown away all of my fountain pens," said Thomas Wickles, one of the first people to purchase a Reynolds Rocket. "I never liked fountain pens. You had to refill the ink every time you wanted to write something, and it always made a big mess." He held up the ballpoint pen with pride. "But *this* is cutting-edge technology!"

Two days ago, Gimbel's placed a full-page ad in the *New York Times* to promote the first sale of ballpoint pens in the United States. The ad guaranteed that the pen will write for two years without a refill—much longer than any fountain pen currently on the market.

American inventor Milton Reynolds is credited as the creator of the Reynolds Rocket, but *Inventor's Times* research shows that a scandal may be afoot. International sources tell us that the ballpoint pen was actually invented several months ago! Its real creators were two brothers in Argentina named Laszlo and Georg Biro.

(continued on page 2)

DID YOU KNOW?

with Guest Expert Etta Mology

The term "pen knife" originated long ago when a special knife was used to sharpen the quill for writing.

IN THIS WEEK'S NEWS

U.S. Government Ends Shoe and Meat Rationing

New Tupperware Containers Are Perfect for Leftovers

Suffragists Win Women's Vote in France

(continued from page 1)

Our sources also explained that Milton Reynolds visited Argentina just four months ago, and purchased several of the Biro brothers' pens. When he returned to America, he started the Reynolds International Pen Company, which sells the Reynolds Rocket.

The Biro Brothers aren't giving up, however. All reports confirm that they will start selling their pens in the United States in the near future, and these Biro pens will compete with the Reynolds Rocket.

COMING NEXT WEEK

Invisible Ink: Will it work with my new ballpoint?

PROTECT YOUR IDEAS!

**Editorial by
Patent Attorney
Madge Istrate, Esq.**

When you patent your invention, the government registers the idea in your name, so you can get credit for it. Since the Biro Brothers didn't patent their invention in the United States, it was very easy for Milton Reynolds to profit from their idea. Don't let this happen to you! Always, always, always patent your ideas! And if you know where to find the Biro Brothers, please give them a copy of this column. It sounds like they could use some good legal advice!

HOW IT WORKS

With Professor Jiminy Snoof, Jr.

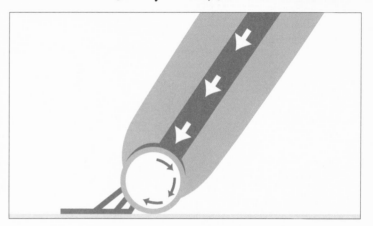

The ball in a ballpoint pen prints its ink onto the paper as it rolls over the paper.

The ink that is used in ballpoint pens is very thick, even thicker than syrup. It is made from oils and dyes. Gravity makes the ink in the pen fall onto the ball as it sits in its socket. As the pen is moved across the paper, the ball turns, and the ink is transferred onto the paper.

Ink Stain Removal

Ballpoints are much neater than fountain pens—but you still might end up with an occasional ink stain. Fortunately, we've developed a way to combat these nasty little spills. We suggest practicing these steps so that you are ready when a real ink stain emergency strikes. Be sure to ask a parent for permission to do this experiment!

MATERIALS:

Old sock (any color but black)
A ballpoint pen
Alcohol-based hair spray
Two rags

1. Use the ballpoint pen to scribble some lines on the old sock.

2. Wet the ink stain with hair spray until it is very moist. Place the rag under the stain to absorb the excess ink.

3. Blot the stain with the other rag. Alcohol-based hairspray is very effective for removing ink stains. Repeat this process until the stain is removed.

4. Wash the old sock. And then wash your hands!

THE INVENTOR'S TIMES

FEBRUARY 16, 1946   VOLUME XCVI NO. 7   PRICE: SIX CENTS

NEW "COMPUTING" MACHINE AMAZES SCIENTISTS!

30-Ton Math Whiz Can Add 5,000 Numbers in One Second!

PHILADELPHIA, PENNSYLVANIA – What weighs 30 tons, solves really hard multiplication problems, and is bigger than your bedroom? No, it's not that really weird kid from your math class who's always eating rubber cement. We're talking about a new invention called the Electronic Numerical Integrator and Computer (friends just call it ENIAC).

The official dedication ceremony for ENIAC was held yesterday at the University of Pennsylvania. The inventors, John Mauchley and J. Presper Eckert, explained that they created the machine to perform lots of math problems very quickly.

If you're wondering how quick and smart ENIAC really is, just try to do the following math problem: What's 8,759,913 multiplied by 9,253,734 multiplied by 8,675,309? The answer is 703,237,071,966,179,278,878 —and ENIAC solved this problem in less than one second.

Unlike calculators of today, which require mechanical relay (moving parts) to solve problems, ENIAC uses electrical currents to transfer information. The result is a "brain" that's incredibly fast. "I've never seen anything like it," remarked Al Gorithim, a mathematics professor who attended the ceremony. "The really exciting news is that Mauchly and Eckert can rewire ENIAC so it can solve many different kinds of problems."

The inventors met at the University of Pennsylvania five years ago, when John Mauchly was 33 and J. Prespert Eckert was only 23. The two men quickly became friends and decided to build

(continued on page 2)

The new ENIAC computer may be the biggest "brain" on Earth.

IN THIS WEEK'S NEWS

New Bikini Swimsuits Are All the Rage in France

Italy Unveils New "Espresso" Coffee Machine

Central Intelligence Agency (CIA) Open for Business

(continued from page 1)

ENIAC together. When the U.S. Army heard about the idea, it provided generous amounts of money to develop the computer.

At the end of the ceremony, everyone applauded the inventors. College freshman Troy Gonometry was among the many people cheering. "I would love to get an ENIAC to help with my math homework," he told us, "but it wouldn't fit in my dorm room!"

WHY UNCLE SAM PAID FOR THE COMPUTER

An Editorial by U.S. Army Drill Sergeant Frank Faulkner

LISTEN UP, you worms, because I don't have a lot of time to waste! The army helped build ENIAC because we knew it could help us make better missiles.

NOW IF YOU THINK LAUNCHING A MISSILE IS EASY, THINK AGAIN! There are thousands of calculations that need to be made. You have to consider speed, weight, wind, trajectory, and hundreds of other factors. It would take a regular person DAYS to figure it out. DO

ANY OF YOU GENIUSES WANT TO TRY IT? NO? I DIDN'T THINK SO! Fortunately, ENIAC can make all the calculations in just three minutes. NOW GET DOWN IN THE MUD AND GIVE ME SOME PUSH-UPS!

These women really know how to push ENIAC's buttons.

DID YOU KNOW?

with Guest Expert Flo P. Disch

Many electronic devices, such as radios, use several vacuum tubes. ENIAC uses over 17,000 vacuum tubes. With each of these tubes working at a rate of 100,000 pulses per second, ENIAC has 1.8 billion opportunities to break down *every second*! So far, the machine appears to be holding up pretty well, but many inventors plan to start working on a new computer that doesn't depend on vacuum tubes. We need a more reliable technology.

ENIAC ☞ VS. ☞ YOU

Face it — you'll never do math as fast as ENIAC, but if you learn some basic math tricks, you can get pretty fast (for a human).

When you multiply numbers that end in zeros, take off the zeros and multiply the numbers that are left. When you get the answer, attach the zeros you removed to the end of the number.

To solve 30 x 40, think 3 x 4 = 12. Now put those two zeros back on, and you get 1,200.

To solve 3 x 500, think 3 x 5 = 15. When you put the zeros back on, you get 1,500.

TRY THESE:

A: 10 x 40

B: 80 x 20

C: 300 x 400

D: 5,000 x 300

E: 30,000,000 x 80

Answers: (A) 400, (B) 1,600, (C) 120,000, (D) 1,500,000, (E) 2,400,000,000

THE 💡 INVENTOR'S TIMES

DECEMBER 1, 1946   VOLUME XCVI NUMBER 48   PRICE: SEVEN CENTS

NEW SLINKY WALKS DOWN STAIRS—ALONE OR IN PAIRS!

"And Makes a Slinkety Sound!" Cheers Inventor

PHILADELPHIA, PENNSYLVANIA–Forget about BB Guns and baby dolls. Never mind bicycles or model train sets. For this year's holiday season, the hottest toy is shaping up to be a strange new invention called "Slinky." Last week, at the Gimbel's department store in Philadelphia, more than 400 Slinkys walked out the door in just 90 minutes.

But what is a Slinky?

The story begins three years ago, when marine engineer Richard James was experimenting with torsion springs. One of the springs fell off his workbench and began flopping around on the deck of his ship.

This amazing toy is coming soon to a store near you.

While most people would have probably just picked up the spring, James clearly had an inventor's instinct. He brought the spring home to his wife, Betty, and said, "I think there might be a toy in this."

With the help of some neighborhood kids, Richard and Betty fine-tuned the product. Then they manufactured 400 Slinkys, which they brought to Gimbel's last week. Richard

(continued on page 2)

LYNN G. WYST

TELLS YOU

WHAT'S IN A NAME

Betty James found the name SLINKY in the dictionary. It means "stealthy, sleek, and sinuous."

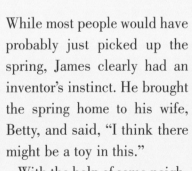

Kids are crazy for Slinky.

IN THE NEWS THIS WEEK

Scientists Make ❄ Artificial Snow from ❆ Real Cloud in Massachusetts

Cadillac Now Has Electric Windows

TWA International Flights Are Really Taking Off

HOW IT WORKS

**With Professor
Jiminy Snoof, Jr.**

Torsion springs have no tension or compression. In other words, they're loose and they don't "spring" back into shape. A Slinky is a torsion spring, and these special properties allow it to "walk."

A Slinky at the top of the stairs has potential energy (energy that is stored and waiting to be released). When you push the Slinky, that potential energy turns into kinetic energy, or motion. As the Slinky falls over, energy travels along the length of the Slinky in a longitudinal wave.

Longitudinal waves can travel along all springs, but most springs are very tightly coiled and stiff, so you can't really see them. Because Slinkys are so loose, we see this longitudinal wave slowly travel along the spring. As the top of the Slinky falls forward and hits the next step, the energy is redirected back along the Slinky, and it begins to "walk" to the next step.

(continued from page 1)

feared that people wouldn't pay money for such a simple toy. He even gave a friend a dollar bill, so that at least one Slinky would be sold. But 90 minutes after their first demonstration, all of the Slinkys were sold out. "It zings and springs!" cried Jane Bartman, age eight. "It's a marvelous thing!"

Now that Slinky is a proven success, Richard is working on a special machine that can twist 80 feet of steel ribbon into plenty of Slinkys for everyone!

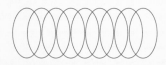

Experiment with Slinky!

Here's a quick experiment you can do with Slinky to demonstrate atmospheric pressure. Stand on a chair with a Slinky and—while holding one end in your hand—let Slinky fall. Once Slinky has extended itself, take notice of the coils. The bottom coils are very close together, because gravity is pulling them toward the Earth. The coils closest to your hand are spaced far apart.

Many astronomers say Slinky would be a very useful on board a rocket ship, so that astronauts could experiment with the toy in zero gravity areas. If you did this experiment in a zero gravity area, how do you think Slinky would respond?

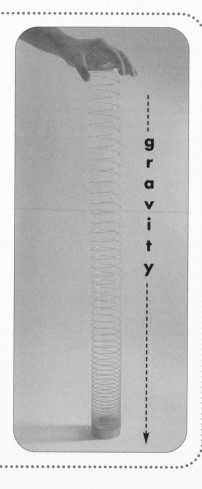

gravity

THE INVENTOR'S TIMES

APRIL 22, 1947   VOLUME XCII NO. 16   PRICE: SEVEN CENTS

CAT OWNERS AGREE: NEW KITTY LITTER IS PURR-FECT!

INVENTOR'S TIMES *HAS THE SCOOP*

Inventor Ed Lowe and his new feline-friendly creation.

CASSOPOLIS, MICHIGAN – Not long ago, 27-year-old Ed Lowe had a plan to expand his family's business. Ed's plan was to sell dried clay to chicken farmers, which they could use as a nesting material. So Ed bought several hundred pounds of dried clay, but when he tried to sell it, none of the local farmers wanted any. Ed was left with more clay than he knew what to do with.

Later in the winter, his next-door neighbor noticed that the sand in her cat's litter box was frozen solid. She couldn't find a substitute that worked. When she tried using ashes from her fireplace, her kitty tracked little black paw prints all over her house.

So Ed Lowe offered her some of his dry clay. After all, he had plenty of it.

It worked so well that the

(continued on page 2)

IN THIS WEEK'S NEWS

Dodgers Sign Jackie Robinson, First Black Man to Play Major League Baseball

Wilks Brothers Release Land Rover in U.K.

"Original Gangster" Al Capone Dies at 48

DID YOU KNOW?

With Guest Expert Harry Lyons

Domestic cats can run faster than humans. A scared cat can run up to 30 miles (48 km) per hour, while the fastest speed ever recorded for a human being is 27.9 miles (44.8 km) per hour.

Lions, tigers, leopards, and jaguars are the only cats that roar.

People have been keeping cats as pets for at least 4,000 years. It is believed that the ancient Egyptians were the first people to welcome cats into their homes.

(continued from page 1)

neighbor came back for more. That's when Ed knew he was onto something. He wrote "Kitty Litter" on ten bags and filled them with the clay. When he brought them to the local pet store, the owner explained that no one would buy "Kitty Litter" for 65 cents since they could get sand for free. So Ed told him to go ahead and give it away for free.

"My cat loves it," exclaims Myra Rutledge, who was one of Ed's first customers. "Kitty Litter is much more absorbent than sand!"

Ed plans to travel to pet stores across the country to demonstrate his product. Will it catch on? Only time will tell. But if this Kitty Litter is popular, we predict that Ed Lowe will capture a lion's share of the market.

HOW TO TOILET TRAIN YOUR CAT

With Professor Jiminy Snoof, Jr.

①   ②   ③

To train a cat to use a litter box, just follow these easy steps.

1. Make sure your kitty has immediate access to the litter box and that she can climb in and out with no extra effort.

2. Watch your kitty closely and place her in the litter box when she wakes up, after meals, or any time she begins nosing in corners or squatting.

3. If your kitty has an accident, wipe it up with a paper towel and place the towel in the litter box. Gently scratch your kitty's front paws in the litter so she learns that this is the place to deposit and bury waste.

4. When your kitty is successful, praise her lavishly!

④

The Many Uses of Kitty Litter

Kitty Litter is a tough, absorbent clay that keeps a cat's litter box dry and odor free. Ed Lowe thought farmers could use it as a nesting material. Can you tell which of the following are real uses for Kitty Litter?

(1) Sprinkle on icy sidewalks, steps, or driveways to make them safer for walking.

(2) Put in the bottom of garbage cans to absorb liquids.

(3) Sprinkle on beaches to add more sand.

(4) Remove fresh spray paint graffiti from sidewalks.

(5) Aid tire traction in icy conditions.

(6) Rub under armpits to get rid of gross body odors.

Answers: 1, 2, 4, 5 are all real uses for Kitty Litter.

We Asked Our Readers

WHICH DO YOU PREFER: KITTY LITTER OR SAND?

Mildred Fusilli, cat-lover, 35: "Let's ask little Shmoopie and see what she likes. Come here, Shmoopie. Yes! That's a good girl! Good girl, Shmoopie! Now does mommy's little Shmoopie like Kitty Litter or sand? Shmoopie? Kitty Litter? Or sand?"

Shmoopie the housecat, 4: "For Pete's sake, someone get this lady away from me. I'm on my ninth life here."

Butch the alley cat, 12: "Kitty Litter, sand, it don't make any difference to me. The world is my litter box."

THE INVENTOR'S TIMES

NOVEMBER 27, 1948   VOLUME XCVIII NO. 48   PRICE: 7 CENTS

INSTANT CAMERA IS PICTURE PERFECT

Edwin Land's Instant Camera Is an Overnight Success

BOSTON, MASSACHUSETTS – Edwin Land claims the inspiration for his new "instant camera" came to him in a picture-perfect moment of clarity. "It was a sunny day in Santa Fe, New Mexico, when my lit-

Inventor Edwin Land, watching his film develop.

tle daughter asked why she could not see at once the picture I had just taken of her. As I walked around the charming town I undertook the task of solving the puzzle she had set me. Within an hour, the camera, the film, and the physical chemistry became so clear to me."

Land's camera will produce an instant photograph within 60 seconds. "When the picture pops out of the camera,

This woman has already taken 20 instant photographs—of herself!

you can watch it come into focus," says amateur photographer Freddy Flank. "It's like the coolest thing I've ever seen."

Freddy Flank isn't the only one who's excited. Mr. Land unveiled his invention—now called the Model 95 Land Camera—at a local department store yesterday. Despite a hefty $89.50 price tag, peo-

ple waited in line to buy this incredible new device.

If you're thinking about getting one, be aware that instant cameras require a special kind of "instant film." Unlike regular film, which must be sent to a darkroom to be developed, instant film can develop itself! That's because it's treated with special chemicals that react

(continued on page 2)

IN THIS WEEK'S NEWS

New York City Subway Fare Jumps to 10 Cents

Scrabble Board Game Is Winning Fans

New 33 1/3 LPs Getting People in the Groove

(continued from page 1)

when they are exposed to light. If you take an instant picture in a dark room, it won't turn out very well.

But customers seem perfectly happy to use their new instant cameras outdoors. "Here, take my picture," Freddy told one of our reporters. "Just push the button. Point and click. Wait, hold on, is my hair okay?"

We Asked Our Readers

Edwin Land's Polaroid camera takes instant photographs. Is this the start of something new? What other instant products would you like to see?

Justin Duckets, Banker, 27: "Money! It's like, maybe you just get this sort of powder and you add water, and wammo! You've got a cool million. Whaddayou say? Do we have a deal?"

Christina Gormay, Homemaker, 35: "How about instant meals, does that sound silly? Maybe food could come in little trays, and I would just heat them up in my oven."

Kyle Grimy, Fifth Grader, 10: "They should make instant showers so I can be clean without having to get wet. I hate taking showers."

INSTANT CAMERA TRICK

Next time you take an instant picture of your friend, grab the photo as soon as it emerges from the camera. Before the picture begins to develop, use a key or another fairly blunt object to draw lines on the photo (the faster you do this, the more effective it will be). When the photo develops, your markings will appear in the image!

DID YOU KNOW

with Guest Expert S. A. Cheez

In 1900, Kodak's Brownie Camera sold for $1.00. The intention was to make cameras available to as many people as possible. The Brownie contained a roll of film with 100 exposures. Once the film was used, the camera and the film were sent back to Kodak, where the film was developed and new film was put into the camera.

THE 💡 INVENTOR'S TIMES

DECEMBER 1, 1952   VOLUME CII NO. 48   PRICE: 7 CENTS

MAN-EATING 3-D LIONS ATTACK MOVIE THEATER

"THEY WERE COMING RIGHT AT ME!" SCREAMS USHER

LOS ANGELES, CALIFORNIA – At 8:47 P.M. last night, two man-eating lions jumped out of a movie screen and attacked patrons at the Melba Theatre. Amazingly, the entire audience escaped unharmed because these lions were part of the first full-length 3-D motion picture, entitled *Bwana Devil*.

"You've never seen anything like it," exclaimed theater manager Roger Fozzilstuff. "Up until now, we've only had short five-minute 3-D movies. But this full-length feature will spark a revolution in entertainment."

To watch a 3-D movie, viewers wear special glasses that

(continued on page 2)

Audiences were horrified by the 3-D lions, but no major injuries were reported.

DID YOU KNOW

with Guest Expert Itza Komenatchu

The Lumiere brothers.

Lots of people take credit for inventing 3-D photography, but everyone agrees on who made the first 3-D movie. The honor goes to Auguste and Louis Lumiere, two brothers in France who helped develop motion picture technology. In 1903, the Lumiere brothers held the first public exhibition of a 3-D movie: *L'Arrivee du Train* (*The Arrival of a Train*). The movie showed a train pulling into a station, and it only lasted ten seconds! Nearly 50 years would pass before filmmakers had the technology and resources to create a full-length 3-D motion picture.

IN THIS WEEK'S NEWS

Jonas Salk on Polio Vaccine: "It Finally Works!"

....

New *TV Guide* Magazine Offers Guide to TV

....

Kids Are Crazy for New Mr. Potato Head

HOW IT WORKS

With Professor Jiminy Snoof, Jr.

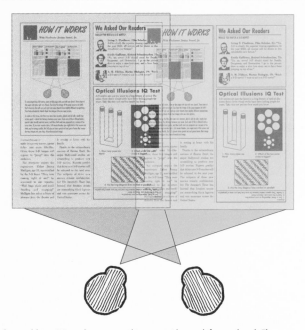

To understand how 3-D works, stare at this page with your left eye closed. Then stare at this page with your right eye closed. See how the image of the page appears to shift? That's because the left eye and right eye view objects from slightly different perspectives. Your brain seamlessly blends these two images into one clear picture.

To make a 3-D movie, the film crew uses two cameras, placed side by side, nearly two inches apart — about the distance between your eyes. Each reel of film is filtered with a special color, usually red and green, and then both reels are projected on a screen at the same time. If you ever wander into a 3-D movie theater, you might look at the screen and think you're seeing double. But 3-D glasses have special red and green lenses that merge the two images into one clear, three-dimensional image.

(continued from page 1)

make images on screen appear fuller and more life-like. Often, these 3-D images will appear to "jump" into the audience.

Not everyone enjoys the experience. Usher Jimmy Mulligan, age 15, was terrified by the 3-D lions: "They were coming right at me!" he screamed to our reporter. "With huge claws and teeth! Snarling and snapping!" Mulligan has taken a leave of absence from the theater and is resting at home with his family.

Thanks to the extraordinary success of *Bwana Devil*, the major Hollywood studios are scrambling to produce new 3-D movies. Experts predict that thirty new 3-D movies will be released in the next year. The subjects of these new movies remain confidential, but *The Inventor's Times* has learned that location scouts are researching black lagoons and wax museums across the United States.

We Asked Our Readers

WOULD YOU WATCH A 3-D MOVIE?

Irving T. Phadimus, Film Scholar, 51: "Yes. 3-D is clearly the superior viewing experience. In the year 2002, all movies will be shown in this remarkable new format."

Estelle Guffleton, Retired Schoolteacher, 75: "No, no, never! 3-D should stand for Deadly, Dangerous, and Destructive. I go to the picture show to enjoy a nice love story, not to have lions jumping on top of me."

A. M. Fibbian, Marine Biologist, 19: "Watch a 3-D movie? I want to *act* in a 3-D movie!"

Optical Illusions IQ Test

3-D movies are just the latest in a long history of optical illusions; these clever visual tricks have been fooling people for years. Take this test and see how much you know.

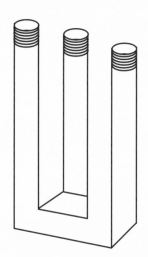

1. How many pipes are there?

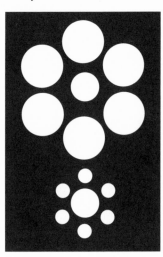

2. Which of the two center circles is bigger?

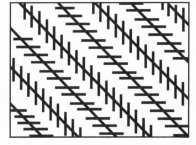

3. Are the long diagonal lines crooked or parallel?

Answers:
1. Two or three, depending on your perspective.
2. They're the same size. Measure them!
3. Parallel. They appear crooked because the cross lines fool your sense of perspective.

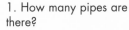

THE INVENTOR'S TIMES

September 21, 1955   Volume CV No. 38   Price: eight cents

DOG HELPS INVENTOR CREATE VELCRO®

MAN'S BEST FRIEND IS NOW A TRUSTED BUSINESS PARTNER

The surface of Mars? No! It's Velcro!

Lynn G. Wyst

TELLS YOU

What's in a Name

VEL + CRO = VELCRO

VEL is from the word *velour*, a plush fabric.

CRO is from the word *crochet*, which is a type of needlework.

SWITZERLAND – What's sharp and prickly on one side, soft and fuzzy on the other, and holds things together? That's right—we're talking about Velcro, the new man-made fastener that inventors everywhere are cheering.

Swiss inventor George de Mestral had the inspiration for Velcro on a beautiful summer day in 1948. He was walking his dog through a series of fields, and when they returned home, he noticed that his pants and his dog's legs were covered with burrs. If you've ever walked in the forest, you've probably had burrs cling to your socks—they are small prickly pods that carry plant seeds.

George spent the next hour removing the burrs from himself and from his dog. He was impressed by how these tiny little burrs clung so tightly to his clothes, so he placed one of

George de Mestral

them under a microscope.

He saw that each burr was coated with many hook-like prickles. These hooks became entangled in the dog's hair,

(continued on page 2)

IN THIS WEEK'S NEWS

Plastic Legos Help Kids Play Well

....

"Disneyland" Theme Park Opens in California

....

Illinois Law Says You Must Wear a Seat Belt

....

HOW IT WORKS

With Professor Jiminy Snoof, Jr.

Every Velcro hook-and-loop fastener has two parts. The first part is a strip with hundreds or even thousands of loops; these loops are so tiny that you'll need a magnifying glass to get a good look at them. The second part is a strip with tiny hooks on it. When these two strips are pressed together, the hooks "grab" the loops, and the fastener is closed!

(continued from page 1)

and they snagged on the loops of thread on George's pants and jacket. George realized that these hooks and loops could be duplicated in a man-made fabric, and this fabric could be used to stick things together.

"I thought George had lost his marbles," says Sven Swanson, one of George's neighbors. "We've already got buttons. We've already got zippers. Why do we need another fastener?"

Despite his critics, George began manufacturing Velcro with the help of Nylon, an inexpensive material that can easily be shaped into tiny hooks. To protect his inven-

tion, George patented his hook-and-loop fastener, and trademarked the name Velcro. He is currently running Velcro Industries, and will sell Velcro to anyone who needs to stick things together.

ARE LAZY PLANTS RIPPING YOU OFF?

An Editorial by Consumer Advocate Penny Pleebo

Since plants can't move around, they depend on animals and the weather to help them spread and reproduce. Take the dandelion, for instance. It has tiny, light seeds that are spread by the wind. Other kinds of plants have seeds that are wrapped in burrs. When these burrs stick on our clothes, we transport them to new locations, so the plants can spread and reproduce. This happens all the time—we're doing all the work, and lazy plants are getting all the benefits! When was the last time plants gave you money for moving their seeds? Probably never! Does this seem fair? I don't think so! I recommend that we all stop walking through forests immediately. You can also write your congressman today and tell him you want to STOP GETTING RIPPED OFF BY LAZY PLANTS!

FAMOUS FASTENERS: HOW DOES VELCRO STACK UP?

METHOD	STAYS TOGETHER?	COMFORTABLE TO WEAR?	COMES APART?
VELCRO	YES	YES	YES
CHEWING GUM & HAIR	YES	NOT REALLY	WITH SCISSORS OR PEANUT BUTTER
MAGNETS	YES	NOT IF YOU HAVE BRACES	YES
TAR & FEATHERS	FOR A LONG, LONG TIME	SURE, BUT YOU LOOK LIKE A REALLY WEIRD CHICKEN	NEVER

THE INVENTOR'S TIMES

October 26, 1955 — Volume CV No. 43 — Price: eight cents

HAPPY HOMEMAKERS ZAP DINNER WITH MICROWAVES

SUPER-FAST OVEN OFFERS A TASTE OF THE FUTURE

MANSFIELD, OHIO – Have you ever found yourself in the kitchen, wishing you could heat a mug of hot chocolate in just 60 seconds? Or cook a melted cheese sandwich in half a minute? Until now, most people didn't have the technology to make these kinds of "instant" meals. But thanks to a new "microwave" oven unveiled yesterday by the Tappan Company, super-fast

cooking is now available to homeowners everywhere.

This microwave oven cooks food without heat—and it cooks fast. It's also the first microwave oven designed for home use. Until now, the only other microwave oven on the market has been the Raytheon Radarange, which costs $3,000 and weighs 750 pounds (340km)!

The Tappan microwave is much cheaper—$1,295, to be exact. And it's only the size of an electric oven. "I'm so excited," gushed Christina Gormay, a mother of three. "I've heard so much about this 'magic cooking.' I can't wait to make popcorn."

But other people, like U.S. Army Drill Sergeant Frank Faulkner, are more skeptical. "Let me tell you something about these microwaves," Sgt. Faulkner shouted at our

Microwave oven inventor Percy Spencer.

reporters. "They don't use heat! They use NUCLEAR POWER! These little ovens are like having a NUCLEAR REACTOR in your kitchen. Now do you want to have a NUCLEAR MELTDOWN while you're eating your Mac and Cheese? Well, do you?!? LOOK AT ME WHEN I'M TALKING TO YOU!"

Here at *The Inventor's Times*, Professor Jimmy Snoof, Jr. assured us that microwave

The Raytheon Radarange.

cooking is actually very safe. "But don't tell Sergeant Faulkner I said so," he told us. "That guy scares the heck out of me."

The compact Tappan microwave.

Percy L. Spencer: FATHER OF THE MICROWAVE OVEN

During World War II, Percy Spencer spent most of his time working with magnetrons, the tubes that produce microwaves. Many days, he was in the lab from morning to night. Sometimes he kept a chocolate bar in his pocket, in case he became hungry.

One day in 1945, while working with a magnetron, he noticed his chocolate had melted—but the room wasn't even warm! Percy suspected that the microwaves had spoiled his snack, so he sent for some popcorn. When he held it front of the magnetron, the popcorn popped!

It looks like this lucky accident is going to make Percy Spencer a very wealthy man. With the success of the microwave oven, he'll be able to buy all the chocolate bars he wants!

HOW IT WORKS

With Professor Jiminy Snoof, Jr.

Microwaving a hot dog is very similar to boiling a hot dog—only the process is reversed. When you boil a hot dog, you place the hot dog in a pot of water and place the pot on a burner. The burner heats the pot, and eventually the water will start to boil. This boiling water will cook the hot dog from the outside-in.

But when you place a hot dog in a microwave oven, the water that is already inside the hot dog absorbs microwaves. To understand this, you need to remember that most foods already contain large amounts of water—celery, for example, is almost 90% water! A hot dog also has plenty of water in it. Microwaves cause these water molecules to become very, very hot—so hot, in fact, that they "cook" anything around it.

INSIDE THE MICROWAVE OVEN

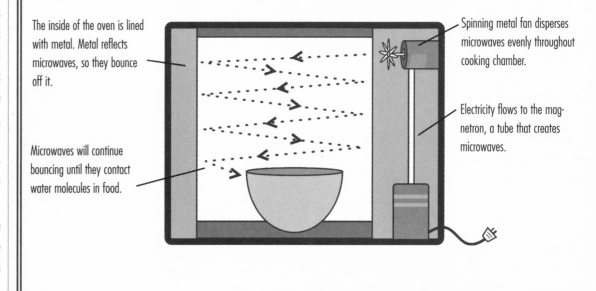

The inside of the oven is lined with metal. Metal reflects microwaves, so they bounce off it.

Microwaves will continue bouncing until they contact water molecules in food.

Spinning metal fan disperses microwaves evenly throughout cooking chamber.

Electricity flows to the magnetron, a tube that creates microwaves.

MICROWAVE RICE KRISPIE TREATS

Here's a quick and easy recipe that you can make with the help of an adult.

Materials:

Microwave oven
1/2 cup butter
5 cups miniature marshmallows
5 cups of crispy rice cereal

1. Put the butter in a 12 x 7-inch glass baking dish. Microwave on medium-high for 1 to 1 1/2 minutes until the butter melts.

2. Stir in the marshmallows and microwave for 1 minute on medium-high.

3. Stir again, then cook for another 1 or 2 minutes, until the marshmallows are soft. Stir the mixture until it is smooth.

4. Mix in the cereal, smooth it out in the pan, then let it cool.

5. Carefully cut the mixture into squares—and then snack away!

WE ASKED OUR READERS

Is microwave cooking in your future?

Francois Clouseau, Chef, 47: "Zee meat does not brown! Zee potatoes does not crisp! I cannot stir zee sauce in zees oven. Zees is not zee art of cooking—zees is science!"

Sally Fluffafloss, Fourth Grader, 9: "No way. My 13-year-old cousin just started working in a restaurant with a microwave. Now hair has started growing on his face, and his voice is getting real deep. I don't want that to happen to me!"

Hamilton G. Shlockfart, Self-Employed, 105: "Why do you people keep asking me questions? Can't I get a little privacy?"

THE INVENTOR'S TIMES

October 21, 1969   Volume CXIX No. 43   Price: 15 cents

NEW ARPA COMPUTERS "SPEAK" TO EACH OTHER

Are Networked Computers the Future of Communication?

LOS ANGELES, CALIFORNIA – Imagine a world where you can speak to someone in Antarctica without picking up the telephone. A world where you can buy a book just by punching a few buttons. A world where you can access an entire library of books just by turning on a screen.

It'll never happen, right?

The Advanced Research Projects Agency (ARPA) believes that it will. This branch of the United States Department of Defense has created a link between computers at several universities that allows them to share information. It's called ARPAnet.

The first-ever computer-to-computer communication happened yesterday. A computer scientist at the University of California, Los Angeles, began typing a message into his computer, and it was transmitted to a computer at Stanford University, more than 300 miles away. The message was intended to be the word "LOGIN," but only the first letter was transmitted before the entire system crashed! Still, many believe this could be the first baby step toward linking computers all over the world.

Here at *The Inventor's Times*, we asked our on-staff psychic,

Researchers at ARPA are communicating via computer.

Magda Pantazopolous, to predict the future of ARPAnet. She immediately closed her eyes and fell into a deep trance. "I see lists of buddies," Magda told us. "And I hear a voice! A man is shouting! He has a message for you. It is very important. He is saying you've got mail. But who is he? Is he from the Post Office? Why does he have your mail?" She opened her eyes and shrugged. "Magda has spoken. She must reveal no more."

We'll keep you posted with more details as this story develops.

IN THIS WEEK'S NEWS

WOODSTOCK: PEACE, LOVE, AND LOTS OF STUFF WE CAN'T PRINT

SONY INVENTS VIDEO-CASSETTE SYSTEM

PEOPLE STILL TALKING ABOUT ARMSTRONG'S MOON WALK

We Asked Our Readers

If you could contact anyone using your computer, who would it be, and what would you say?

Mr. X, International Spy, Age Classified: "I'm sorry, but my contacts are top-secret classified information. If I told you, I would have to kill you."

Simone Freebird, Student Activist, 19: "I'd send a song about the love between my brothers and my sisters all over this land."

Al Gore, Student, 21: "I just want to be very clear that the Internet was really my idea—all mine. So I'd probably contact a bunch of people to let them know."

HOW IT WORKS

With Professor Jiminy Snoof III

Within the next 25 to 30 years, individual computers will be able to connect to networks called Internet Service Providers (or ISPs for short). I'm fairly confident that the world will have many ISPs of varying sizes. Your computer will be armed with the address of a particular machine, and it will navigate the many ISPs until it finds its destination.

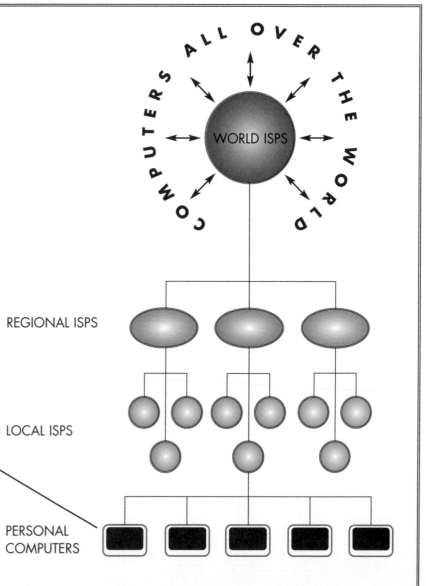

COMPUTERS ALL OVER THE WORLD

WORLD ISPS

REGIONAL ISPS

LOCAL ISPS

PERSONAL COMPUTERS

THE INVENTOR'S TIMES

November 15, 1972   Volume CXXII No. 46   Price: 15 cents

"PONG" VIDEO ARCADE GAME IS A HIT WITH KIDS!

State-of-the-Art Graphics Dazzle Fans Everywhere

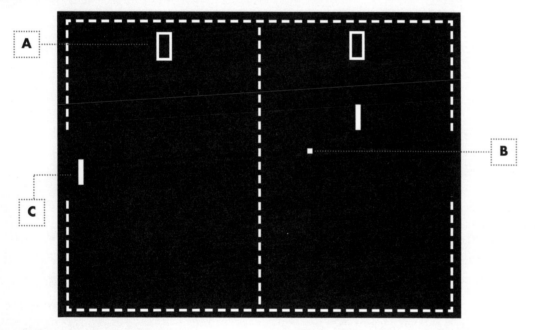

Nolan Bushnell relaxes after a long game of Pong.

A) SCORE: Players score one point when their opponent misses a serve.

B) WHITE DOT: Ball that bounces across screen.

C) WHITE LINES: Paddles controlled by players.

SUNNYVALE, CALIFORNIA – Just one day after installing Pong, a coin-operated arcade game, at a popular pool parlor in Sunnyvale, California, 28-year-old inventor Nolan Bushnell received a phone call explaining that his new machine was broken.

However, when Bushnell showed up to fix the problem, he was pleasantly surprised. The reason no one could play the game was because the machine was stuffed full of quarters!

"I had three quarters lined up on the machine," said Kathleen Hatch, a ninth grade hooligan who was cutting class to play Pong. "So I was pretty glad when Mr. Bushnell fixed the machine. At that point, who could go back to pinball?"

Kathleen's boyfriend, Billy

(continued on page 2)

(continued from page 1)

Swift, agreed. "Pinball is, like, so yesterday."

Pong is a video game version of ping-pong. The ball is a small white dot that bounces between two paddles. The paddles are moved by the players, who use control devices located on the machine.

Bushnell predicts that coin-operated video games are going to be a great success. Last year, we reported that Bushnell invented the first coin-operated video game, which was called "Computer Space." Unfortunately, that game had so many rules and complicated controls that most people just couldn't understand it. So Bushnell knew that his next video game was going to be extremely simple.

"Pong is very easy to learn," Kathleen Hatch agreed. "And the graphics are awesome!"

Bushnell has already earned $500 from the success of Pong, and he is planning to start a small video game com-

Sure, Pong is fun—but more fun than pinball?

pany called Atari. "The critical ingredient is getting off your butt and doing something," he advised inventors earlier this morning. "It's as simple as that. A lot of people have ideas, but there are few who decide to do something about them now. Not tomorrow. Not next week. But today. The true entrepreneur is a doer, not a dreamer."

TEST YOUR VIDEO GAME KNOWLEDGE

Are the following statements true or false?

(1) A committee for the Olympics has decided that Pong will replace ping-pong at the next Olympics.

(2) The only instructions on Pong read "Insert quarter, avoid missing ball for high score."

(3) Nolan Bushnell originally wanted to call his company Syzygy instead of Atari.

(4) Before making Pong, Nolan Bushnell created a video game that no one liked called Computer Space.

(5) The highest score you can get on Pong is 100.

(6) If Pong players score more than 100 points, the game dispenses a free stuffed animal.

(7) If players get bored of playing Pong, the machine also functions as a giant electronic Etch-a-Sketch.

Answers: (1) F (2) T (3) T (4) T (5) F (6) F (7) F

WE ASKED OUR READERS

What Will Pong Replace in Your Life?

Real ping-pong	31%
Watching television	19%
Dating	20%
Pinball	17%
Reading	13%

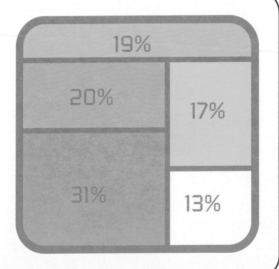

The Inventor's Times

October 2, 1982   Volume CXXXII No. 40   Price: 20 cents

NEW COMPACT DISCS USE LASERS TO PLAY MUSIC

But will they really replace records and 8-track tapes?

TOKYO, JAPAN – When he was six years old, James T. Russell made his first invention: a remote-controlled battleship with a storage chamber to hold his lunch. Now, 45 years later, he has unveiled an invention that may change the way you hear music: the compact disc (CD) player.

Russell, a physicist, invented CDs because he loved music and wanted to find a better recording device than vinyl records. If you have a phonograph, you already know it has a needle that rubs against the record and "picks up" the sound. But records can wear out after extended use, and they have poor sound quality if they are scratched or dusty.

Russell's idea was to develop a system that didn't use a needle to play audio. He want-

Compact disc inventor and music lover James T. Russell.

ed to try using light to read the data on a disc. More than 15 years would pass before Russell's invention was fully developed (and he'd file 22 patents along the way!).

But these discs can store more than just your favorite Van Halen album. Experts claim that compact discs can hold all different kinds of information—books, maps, photographs, maybe even movies!

And the inventor himself is

Inside the new CD player.

heading back into the workshop. "I've got hundreds of ideas stacked up," Russell said. "Many of them worth more than the compact disc."

IN THIS WEEK'S NEWS

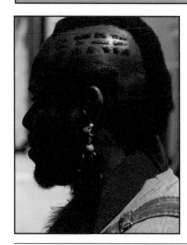

E.T. the Extra-Terrestrial Is Out of This World

Mr. T Is Ready to Star on *The A-Team*

Patient with Artificial Heart Still Going Strong

HOW IT WORKS

 With Professor Jiminy Snoof III

ACRYLIC LAYER:
The top layer of the CD, where the label is printed.

MICROSCOPIC BUMPY LAYER:
The information on compact discs is stored in millions of microscopic bumps. When the laser hits the shiny aluminum layer, it bounces off and hits an optical reader. The size and spacing of the little bumps change the way the laser bounces—and the optical reader interprets these changes as information.

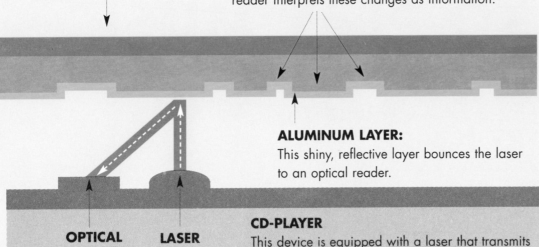

ALUMINUM LAYER:
This shiny, reflective layer bounces the laser to an optical reader.

OPTICAL READER

LASER

CD-PLAYER
This device is equipped with a laser that transmits information to a special optical reader.

HOW TO CLEAN YOUR COMPACT DISCS

Although music manufacturers claim that CDs will supply you with "Perfect Sound, Forever," we here at *The Inventor's Times* have heard some strange noises coming from our new CD player. It turns out that our CDs were a little dusty—but a sink full of soapy water fixed the problem. Here's how you can keep your CD collection in tip-top shape.

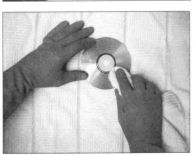

MATERIALS:

> **Any malfunctioning CDs**
> **A soft cloth**
> **Soft hand soap**
> **A sink full of water**

1. Fill up your sink with some soapy water.

2. Dip your CDs in the soapy water.

3. Wipe them dry with a soft cloth. Always clean the disc from the center working outward. Do not use any scrubbers with a rough surface, like Brillo Pads or Porcupine Skins.

4. Allow CDs to dry completely.

5. Play that funky music!

The Inventor's Times

November 21, 1983   Volume CXXXIII No. 47   Price: 25 cents

NEW "MOUSE" CONTROLS COMPUTERS

But Will It Click With Computer Geeks?

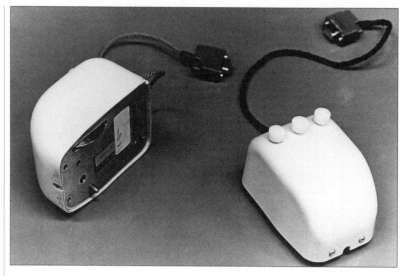

EEK! This mouse makes computing easy.

UNITED STATES – Sometimes creating an invention is the easy part—and finding the right name is difficult. Back in 1968, inventor Douglas Engelbart wowed spectators when he demonstrated his "X-Y Position Indicator for a Display System." It wasn't a very catchy name, but the invention itself was quite impressive. Using a small device that he pushed around a flat surface, Engelbart could give commands and instructions to a computer.

For the last 15 years, Engelbart's invention could only be found in computer labs or with advanced office equipment. But Apple Computer recently announced that its newest home computer, nicknamed Lisa, will come packaged with an "X-Y Position Indicator for a Display System." Only they've decided to call this device a "mouse."

"It looks a little like a mouse," says our own Professor Snoof, who recently broke open a device to under- stand how it works (see side- bar, p. 2). "I bet it'll change the way people interact with computers. You'll do less typ- ing, and more pointing and clicking."

This amazing invention was inspired by a boring lecture. "One day I was watching somebody talk at a conference that just wasn't interesting to me," Engelbart said. "I started thinking about gadgets. I began to recollect interesting things I'd seen in the laborato- ry." Pretty soon, Engelbart had sketched out his mouse, and

(continued on page 2)

Inventor Douglas Engelbart.

IN THIS WEEK'S NEWS

Sales of Cabbage Patch Kids Approach 3 Million

Michael Jackson's *Thriller* **CD Sparks Moonwalk Craze**

Interview with Sally Ride, First Woman in Space

(continued from page 1)

then he asked an engineer to build it. Now that Apple is mass-producing mice for home use, it seems like this invention is poised to take off.

But even if it doesn't, Engelbart still has plenty of other great ideas—including a five-key typewriter where each button stands for more than one letter, and a system where people can send "mail" from one computer to another. Somebody get this man a patent lawyer!

HOW IT WORKS

With Professor Jiminy Snoof, III

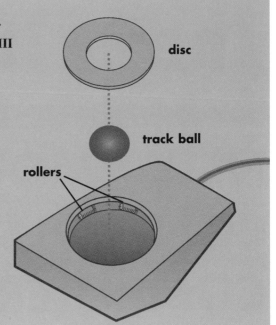

If you can get your hands on a mouse, it's easy to see how it works. The bottom of the mouse is equipped with a small rubber ball that makes it easy to roll on a flat surface. (There should be a tiny disc on the bottom of the mouse; slide it off and the ball will pop out.) You'll see that two tiny rollers are placed against the ball; one records movement in the X (left-right) direction, and the other records movement in the Y (up-down direction). When you push the mouse, the ball rolls, and one or both of the rollers will start to spin. These rollers will send information to your computer, which translates the data into coordinates.

UNDERSTANDING HOW A MOUSE WORKS

A mouse records its movements using an X-Y Coordinate plane. This plane is similar to a grid with a horizontal and vertical axis. The X-coordinate refers to a point on the horizontal line, and the Y-coordinate refers to a point on a vertical line. Whenever you see a pair of coordinates, the X-coordinate is always given first.

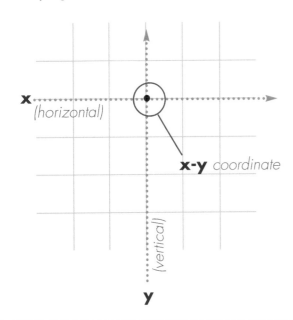

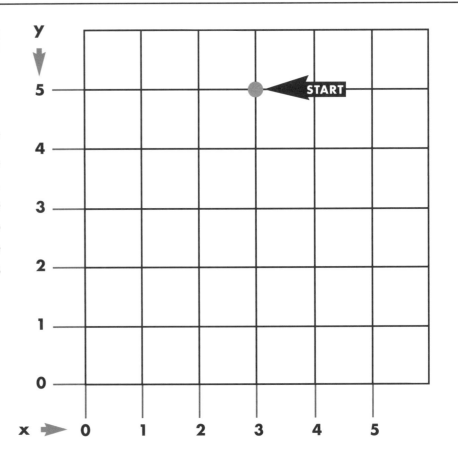

Copy this grid onto a sheet of paper. You'll see that we've already marked the first dot at coordinate **(3,5)**.

Starting there, place a dot at the next coordinate, and connect them with a line. When you're finished, what shape are you left with?

(3,5): START
(4.5,1)
(1,4)
(5,4)
(1.5,1)
(3,5)

The Inventor's Times

Visit us on the web at: www.quirkproductions.com/inventors.html

Tuesday, June 2, 1999   Volume IC Number CLXVII $1.00

IN THIS WEEK'S NEWS

Star Wars: Episode 1 Is Major Force at Box Office

Dolly, the First Cloned Sheep, Is *Baaack* on Her Feet

New Superstar Ricky Martin is Livin' La Vida Loca

NEW ROBOT DOG PERFORMS OLD TRICKS

But Is This Cyber Canine the Pet of the Future?

YOKAHAMA, JAPAN – More than 2,000 people placed orders on the Internet yesterday for AIBO, a new robotic dog manufactured by the Sony Corporation. The name AIBO stands for "Artificial Intelligence roBOt", but it is also the Japanese word for "pal."

In a press release, Sony announced, "Our purpose in developing AIBO is to bring humans and robots closer together. We have done this by creating an artificial being as close to a living creature as possible."

AIBO looks and behaves like a real dog. It can recognize humans, hear commands, chase a ball, bark at other animals, and perform tricks. AIBO can also "learn" if its owner spends time with it. As the dog becomes "older," it performs more advanced tricks and makes fewer mistakes.

The new AIBO owners are eager to receive their pets. "A real dog needs lots of love and attention, and I have to work 12 hours a day," explained corporate executive Norio Hara. "AIBO is the perfect pet

(continued on page 2)

Robot AIBO plays with a friend at a recent technology fair.

GREAT DOGS IN HISTORY					
How AIBO Measures Up	Learns Tricks	Survives without Food	Rescues People in Danger	Good with Children	Fights Red Baron
LASSIE	Yes	No	Yes	Yes	No
SNOOPY	Yes	No	Yes	Yes	Yes
AIBO	Yes	Yes	No	Yes	No

(continued from page 1)

for me. It plays with me at night, and when I go to work, I just recharge its batteries." Hara also points out that AIBO does not shed hair, chew on furniture, or poop on his carpet.

The price of a new AIBO is $2,500. That means a teenager in a fast-food restaurant would have to work ten hours every week for a year (and save every penny!) to buy an AIBO. But despite the high price tag, more than 2,000 AIBOs were sold in just 20 minutes!

"I just told daddy I wanted it," says nine-year-old Veruca Salt. "And as soon as I get my AIBO, I'm going to put it in a room with my diamond tiara, my autographed Britney Spears guitar, and my golden ticket from the Wonka Factory."

ANATOMY OF A ROBO-DOG

The Sony Corporation developed this early prototype of AIBO two years ago. It's not as cute or as smart as the final product, but it still performs 40 different tricks!

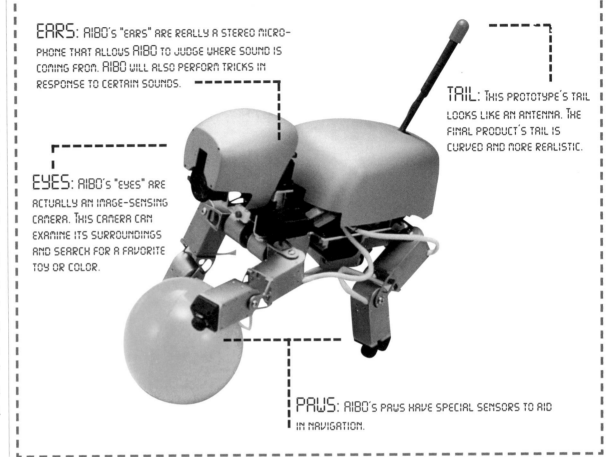

EARS: AIBO'S "EARS" ARE REALLY A STEREO MICRO-PHONE THAT ALLOWS AIBO TO JUDGE WHERE SOUND IS COMING FROM. AIBO WILL ALSO PERFORM TRICKS IN RESPONSE TO CERTAIN SOUNDS.

EYES: AIBO'S "EYES" ARE ACTUALLY AN IMAGE-SENSING CAMERA. THIS CAMERA CAN EXAMINE ITS SURROUNDINGS AND SEARCH FOR A FAVORITE TOY OR COLOR.

TAIL: THIS PROTOTYPE'S TAIL LOOKS LIKE AN ANTENNA. THE FINAL PRODUCT'S TAIL IS CURVED AND MORE REALISTIC.

PAWS: AIBO'S PAWS HAVE SPECIAL SENSORS TO AID IN NAVIGATION.

HOW TO PATENT YOUR INVENTION

If you've been a loyal reader of *The Inventor's Times* over the years, perhaps you've wondered how you can patent your own invention. Take it from the Biro Brothers, who invented the ballpoint pen—if you have a great idea, it's important to protect it!

You can protect your ideas with the help of your government's Patent Office, but only if your invention meets the following guidelines. It must be:

Useful: Your invention has to have a purpose. If you invent something that nobody needs—like a machine that squirts mustard onto sweaters while making a duck sound—then you probably won't get a patent.

Novel: This means that your invention has to be unique, or one-of-a-kind. If the Patent Office knows that a similar invention already exists, then they won't give you a patent.

Non-obvious: You can't just take a wheel, attach it to a computer, and say, "Hey, I've invented a rolling computer!"

The Patent Office has much love for real inspiration, and they don't want to waste time with smart-alecks.

If your invention meets those requirements, you can get a patent, and in most countries it will last for ten to twenty years. Unfortunately, you'll also have to pay a fee for this service, and it can sometimes amount to a large sum of money. But if you've created a good invention, it might be worth it!

A special note to all of you writers, artists, and musicians: If you've created a story, a song, or a work of art, then you'll want to copyright your work, not patent it. Copyrights keep people from copying somebody else's work without permission. In most countries, you can establish a copyright simply by writing "Copyright [year] [your name]" on the actual work.

Your local government should have more information. Good luck, and happy inventing!

✱   ✱   ✱   ✱   ✱   ✱   ✱